I0407525

MIDDLE-CLASS REVOLUTION

The Fight to Take Back Our Government

By Vernon Grossman-Orr

Visit us at MiddleClassRevolution.net

This book is dedicated to Mareida,

my lovely, wonderful, absolutely amazing

wife and very best friend for over 25 years.

ACKNOWLEDGEMENTS

I would like to express my deepest appreciation to my editors.   They were both terrific and easy to work with. They are independent contractors and I highly recommend them. They do excellent work and deliver it on time with a very quick turnaround.

Beatrice Ada (BeatriceAda@gmail.com) or she can be reached at Fiverr.com where her moniker is "beatriceada"

Sarah Pennington who can be reached at Fiverr.com where her moniker is "proofread_book".

I would also like to recognize the artist who designed my cover and the logo on our website.   Her name is Les Solot. She can be reached at Fiverr.com where her moniker is "germancreative." Les is terrifically talented and a real pleasure to work with. She took my concept and a bare minimum of prompts and created a cover and a logo of which I am very proud.

Without the help of all three of these wonderful ladies, I could not have produced this book. I cannot say enough good things about them and I deeply appreciate their help

TABLE OF CONTENTS

CHAPTER 1 - CLASS WARFARE

Can I ask you a question?

If we are driving home from work one afternoon, look up and see the sky littered with paratroopers jumping out of foreign military planes, what will we likely do?

My guess is we get on our phones and start to alert everyone we know that something very ominous is taking place. We may hit the mental panic button. We likely will stop traffic, wave and scream to get everyone's attention and point to the sky.

Well, I've come to realize that, unnoticed by almost everyone, something is going on that could potentially be more dangerous and more devastating to our nation than even such an overt invasion.

This book is me, stopping traffic, waving and screaming with all the force I can muster to get everyone's attention. I believe something quite foreboding is taking place right under our noses, it is so subtle that it goes almost unnoticed, and if we don't do something about it, the consequences can be pretty grave.

Please let me explain.

My name is Vernon Grossman-Orr, and I drive a truck for a living. I am as "average middle-class Joe" as it gets. I am reasonably intelligent, hardworking, honest, live in a modest home, pay my taxes, send my kids to public schools, want opportunities for my family, and care about my country.   I live a pretty busy middle-class life. Odds are, I am a lot like you.

The purpose of my short book is to tell you why I am deeply concerned about where America's middle class is headed. Then, if we agree that things need to be changed, ask for help to create that change, and quickly.

What is happening is so subtle I doubt most of us even realize the problem or its significance.   I know I didn't . But while doing a little research on a entirely different matter, I stumbled onto a piece of information that is deeply disturbing.   This one little piece of information proves unequivocally that, no enemy invasion is necessary, there is already a war going on within the United States.   It is a class war.   I don't think it was started intentionally, but it is happening and we, the middle class/ working class families in our country are getting the hell beat out of us. Furthermore, if we don't do something about it while we can, the fate of the middle class is perilous at best.

Calling it war seems harsh, but I don't know what else to call it.   It is an all-out "us versus them" conflict, and without even realizing it, we are losing badly.   This is the equivalent of being down three touchdowns late in the fourth quarter of a football game.   If we are going to do something, we need to start making it happen.

There are volumes of reliable information available that detail the plight of our middle class, how much better the richest 10% of our country are doing than the bottom 90%, how middle-class income growth is virtually where it was 30 or more years ago, and how we are having to work harder than ever to maintain that level.   None of that really screams "RED ALERT," or seems to give us a real reason to worry.   That may be because most people are like me and don't really care how much the rich make. They only care that, for the most part, we seem to be getting by OK.

But what I am about to show you is compelling evidence that we really are NOT getting by OK.   This piece of information hit me like a solid gut punch.   Since seeing it, I literally have not been able to stop tossing it around in my head.   We are facing a major problem that is quickly becoming a national crisis.

Let me share with you what I have found, and we will see what you think.

In the 1970's, the wealthiest 10% of our population owned about one-third of the entire wealth of our country.   The remaining 90% of us shared the other two-thirds with the poorest 20% owning only a tiny fraction of our total wealth

In 2017, the wealthiest 10% of our population hold a whopping 90% of all of the wealth of our nation!   The remaining 90% of us now only share the remaining 10%.

Take a hard look at that.   Think about it for a minute. In forty or so years, the wealthiest of the wealthy have tripled their share of our entire nation's "economic pie" while our middle-class share has been REDUCED by 85%!

And the rate of transfer is now faster than ever and increasing, mostly due to consumer and credit card debt. Our newly elected President along with his billionaire cabinet and a Republican-controlled Congress seem determined to increase the transfer rate even more.

So, I have to ask myself, how does this play out? What happens in the final chapter?

Wealth is obviously moving from the less rich toward the already rich. The poor already do not have any wealth to speak of, so that means the wealth must be flowing from the middle class.

So here is a question worth consideration. Please think carefully about this.

Wealth is moving from the less wealthy toward the already very rich. The rate of movement has accelerated and continues to increase. What happens if the trend continues? What happens to the middle class?

I don't know exactly what the final picture will look like, but I am absolutely certain it will not be good news for the middle class.

America's total wealth is a finite number. It is a huge number, but it is limited. So, if fewer and fewer people are taking control of more and more of that number at a faster and faster pace, what does that mean for the rest of us?

Now, I don't consider myself to be an alarmist or a "gloom and doomer", but it seems to me that if we don't make some changes, simple logic dictates that we are likely looking at the extinction of the middle class and in a relatively short period of time. Does that make sense to you?

I personally don't care that the rich keep getting richer, but I DO care deeply when it looks like they want to take it ALL, and there's none left for those of us who form the backbone of this country. Unfortunately, that seems to be exactly where we are, and honestly, it is a very scary place to be.

As far as possessions and wealth go, I have very little, not even chump change by the standards of the wealthy. However, when what little I have, and have worked very hard to get, becomes threatened, it becomes personal. My purpose for writing this book is to convince you to take it personally, too.

If we remove the middle class, we only have rich and poor. If we only have rich and poor, we become another Russia, or China, or any number of other nations where there are only rich and poor. Those seem to be the stakes under consideration, and the window of opportunity to change it is getting smaller by the minute.

Let me tell you, I've been poor, and when you are poor, life does not offer you many choices or very much opportunity. Life is hard. Life beats you down a lot. So if we are headed toward a society that has only rich and poor, and that seems to me to be the inescapable conclusion of the current trend, if we aren't rich enough that we are going to come down on the rich side of the divide, then we all need to sit up and pay attention, because being poor sucks.

I don't care which political stripe you wear. If the middle class disappears, it will affect Democrats, Republicans, and people with no political affiliation. Politics will simply not matter. Basically, EVERY family earning less than $250,000 a year should be concerned. This problem is MUCH, MUCH bigger and more urgent than any political divide. If we let the middle class disappear, then America as we know it, ceases to exist. I hope you get that.

And please understand, the kind of change that will occur will be very much like getting to where we already are. It will be subtle, quiet and economically deadly. There will be no big announcement, no fanfare, no flashy advertising, and no warning.   We just wake up one morning and find that the options and choices we had when we went to bed simply do not exist anymore.

For instance, what if your landlord sells the building or space you lease to operate a business, and the new owner triples or quadruples the rent?   Or what if a competitor buys out a major supplier and either makes products needed to operate a business unaffordable or unavailable altogether?   There are literally millions of possibilities where those who have a lot of money can come along and take advantage of those of us who don't.

I believe we are on an economic raft floating lazily down a river headed toward a mighty, crushing waterfall, and don't even realize it.   So, I am trying my best to sound an alarm and get your attention.

WAKE UP!   Take a look around while we can still change course and let's get busy making some changes.

This book is my attempt to explain what I see happening and to ask you to help me start a grassroots movement to help strengthen our middle class and expand the opportunities that being part of the middle class affords, rather than allow it to continue to dwindle into oblivion.

Let me start by asking you a question.   We hear and talk a lot about what a great nation we have, and we DO have a great, powerful nation.   What do you think it is that makes America great?   Think about it for a minute.   We have many things of which we can be proud.   But what single thing makes us the envy of the world?

I think, when broken down to a single statement, the largest contributing factor to our greatness is that we have a strong, functional middle class. Our middle class is where people of all backgrounds and variabilities have opportunities to live a lifestyle that allows choices. The ability to make choices is what makes our nation attractive to people from all around the world who have never had choices.

In large parts of the world, if we are not born rich, we never have the choice or the opportunity to be anything but poor. In this country, we allow people, all kinds of people, regardless of age, education level or ethnicity, the opportunity to make choices that can improve their financial condition and then almost every aspect of their lives. The dream that every immigrant brings to America is that, in America, we all have the chance to be something other than poor. That, I believe is the source, the very heart of the greatness we claim.

From the middle class, we can choose better education, afford home ownership if we want to own a home, drive comfortable automobiles, wear nice clothing, receive decent health care, and have disposable income which we can invest or use to reach out and help others, and do a plethora of things that the poor don't get to enjoy. I know. As I said, my family and I have been poor. Making it to the middle class was a hard-fought journey, and it's such a different life, I don't know if I could ever describe it. But, believe me when I say that being able to have choices is a wonderful thing.

Almost everyone who manages to move from poor to anything close to rich must pass through the middle class. If the middle class goes away, so does all the opportunity it affords. And folks, our middle class is taking a beating. It is shrinking. The standard of living is ebbing. We now have to work harder than ever just to maintain our lifestyle. In terms of comparable dollars, the overall standard of our middle class has changed very little in the last 35 years.

Today's middle class has fewer choices and fewer opportunities and it has less influence over our own destiny than most of us have seen in our lifetimes. Further, for the first time since the Great Depression, in 2017 our children have only a 50% chance of being financially better off than we are. If we don't make some dramatic changes, and soon, even that 50/50 chance of economic improvement goes away.

Most of us have been raised to believe that we live in a democracy where our vote counts and we get to help decide the direction of our nation. I want to warn you that such is NO LONGER the case. I believe if you take a closer look you will understand why. As I will show you as we proceed through my book, we are much less a nation "of the people, by the people and for the people," and are much more a nation "of the rich, by the rich and for the rich." Furthermore, the divide is growing FAST. This is not something that is "About to happen." THIS IS HAPPENING NOW. As we progress through the book, I will show you how the rich ALREADY control almost every aspect of your life, likely without you even noticing.

Now, I don't hate the wealthy and I don't think they hate us (though I personally believe that to we may be viewed by some as just a necessary nuisance). Wealth can be a good thing and aspiring to be wealthy can lead to great accomplishments. But I will say again, if we just think about the logical conclusion to this trend, more and more to fewer and fewer, the end of the story cannot be good news for those of us in the middle class.

So, let me ask you another question.

This trend has been steadily growing and accelerating for decades. Do you think the very rich, who want to keep getting richer, are suddenly going to change their views, and reverse the process?

Perhaps, on about the same day that China petitions Congress to become our 51st state.

Well, do you think that, as our financial resources continue to decrease, our political clout and the power of our voices will increase?

Do you see why this matter is URGENT?

Think about it this way. Let's say there is a huge lake. We will call it Lake Wealth. It provides water, and thus livelihood to millions of people. But a few individuals start hoarding water. They even build their own lakes to store water so they can enjoy their water sports privately, but they take their water from Lake Wealth leaving less water for everyone else. The few keep building bigger and bigger reservoirs and keep demanding more and more of the water from Lake Wealth. That leaves less and less is left for the rest of us who make up the majority. So, if the trend continues and goes unchecked, what happens to Lake Wealth?

All the Lake Wealth resources and benefits end up in the hands of the few and dry up for everyone else.

For those of you unfamiliar with the term, we are talking about an oligarchy.   It is a society where there is a rich, powerful ruling class, and then everyone else. Nothing in between.   If you want to study it up close, just do a little research on Russia.   People in Russia do what the tiny wealthy class who rule tell them to do, period.   Is that what we want for America?   That is certainly where we are headed.

Middle class is where I live.   Middle class is where I want my kids to grow up.   Middle class is a huge source of opportunity in this country and offers the potential to do amazing things.   If it shrinks or disappears, so do all the benefits.   And if we let our country become a rich/poor society, then we will not be the country that people risk their lives to enter and join.   We will more likely become another country where people risk their lives to leave.

Does that make sense?   I hope you are paying attention! We are talking about the future of our families.   Even if the extremely wealthy do not take it ALL, do we really want to offer our families less and less, just the crumbs that remain? Well, if we don't wake up and do something, I am absolutely convinced that is where we all are headed.

There is some good news, or at least potentially good news. We have two advantages.   The first is that we, the working class, seriously outnumber the very rich.   The second is that we, at least for now, have votes that we can use to make needed changes.   However, as I'll show you later, votes from middle-class America do not carry nearly as much weight with our elected officials as votes from the wealthy.   A relative handful of very wealthy individuals already largely dictate how we live in this country, as you will see as you continue through this book.   But the numbers do still matter, and we have enough power left to change things if we will get moving.

In order to be effective, we have to determine first to use our votes, and secondly, we have to be committed to using them in a way that has a positive impact, not just on our personal lives, but to make changes that are good for ALL the middle class and therefore, our nation.

This brings us to the focal point of my book and this entire discussion: the United States Congress.

As an introduction to that topic, let me ask you another question.

If you are a hard-working, middle-class American, whether rural or urban, do you think your federal government SHOULD represent and work for your interests? Certainly! Right? That is what every one of us has been brought up to believe.

Well, do you think your federal government DOES represent and work for your interests?

I doubt you will answer yes, and if you do, I would have to believe you are likely pretty naive. As I will show you in subsequent chapters, unless you are a "top 10% member" that notion is pretty laughable. In the pages that follow, I believe you will see how that the chance of the middle class receiving any relief from Congress, as it now exists, is absolutely ZERO.

Let me give you just a few quick examples of why I say that.

Did you know that recent surveys show that 73% of Americans want the minimum wage raised to $10/hour?

73%!   Almost three-fourths of us! Yet Congress won't make that happen.

Did you know that 68% of Americans want amnesty and a path to citizenship for most illegal aliens working in this country?   Over two-thirds of us want this! Yet, Congress won't make that happen either.

Did you know that 85 percent of Americans say we need to either "Completely rebuild" or make "fundamental changes" to the campaign finance system? Just 13 percent think "Only minor changes are necessary." Yet when was the last time you heard of Congress opening the floor for suggestions on campaign reform?

The truth is, they won't even DISCUSS it because the ideas get killed in committees before they even get introduced to the General Assembly.   How that happens is covered a little later in the book, but for now, just know that the will of the people is being completely ignored.

The actions and attitudes of our current Congress tell us loudly and clearly that Congress DOES NOT CARE about the "will of the people."

And those are just three issues.   There are dozens more.

Doesn't that make you ask yourself HOW, in a country whose government is supposed to be "OF the people, BY the people, and FOR the people," does that happen?   How do less than ten percent of the population have almost absolute control over the laws that affect us all?

Doesn't it make you angry that your vote really doesn't count?   It makes me MAD, livid in fact, that the people who take an oath to promote the general welfare of the entire nation would so ignore our wishes and therefore abuse our trust.   I hope I can make you angry, too.   Maybe if I can get you angry enough, we can get some things done.

We CAN change this situation if we are committed and persistent, but we have to be extremely committed and persistent, AND I believe we have to start NOW. The change will not come easily.

If the rich and powerful, the people who run our government, gave a damn about the middle class, things would not be where they are.   I am certain the middle class can expect absolutely no help from Washington nor the ultra-rich who keep them elected.   If help was coming, we would see signs of it by now.   If you are expecting good things from Washington for the middle class, you may as well be sitting in the middle of the Bonneville Salt Flats with a fishing pole expecting to catch a fish.   And I will demonstrate that to you beyond any doubt in subsequent chapters.

Help from the middle class is ONLY going to come from the middle class.   It also seems inevitable to me that if we don't use our political advantage while we have it, we lose it.   Just as our physical muscle withers from disuse, so it is with our political muscle. If we don't use it while we can, it will shrink until it no longer functions.   If our votes versus their votes don't count with Congress now, how much sway do you think our voices will have when the 10% own 99% or more of all of the available wealth in our nation?

Let me remind you of something.

Remember this?   "We the People of the United States, in Order to form a more perfect Union, establish Justice, insure domestic Tranquility, provide for the common defense, promote the general Welfare, and secure the Blessings of Liberty to ourselves and our Posterity, do ordain and establish this Constitution for the United States of America."

It is, of course, the preamble to our Constitution.   It is the very cornerstone of our greatness.   Every member of Congress swears an oath to uphold the Constitution which clearly includes promoting the general welfare... that is EVERYONE'S welfare, and secure the Blessings of Liberty to ourselves and our Posterity... again, that is for ALL of us.

I believe that EVERY person in Congress has violated that oath and will point out why in the chapters that follow.   I also believe that in doing so, they have and continue to undermine the middle class and thus put at risk everything for which this country stands.

We have ignored and tolerated this behavior, refusing to do anything about it for a very long time, but if you look again at those figures of how fast wealth is being drained from the middle class, it does not take a genius to see that we just cannot afford to tolerate it any longer.   To do so is to literally risk extinction, and soon... likely in our generation, if not, certainly the next.

Changing this trend will not be easy.   It will require a lot of "heavy lifting".   But we need to lift heavy.   We need to rise to the challenge and commit to doing what is necessary to effect real change.

This book explains some of the problems we face, attempts to peel away some of the complexities, and offers a simple, though daunting, solution for how we, the people, can still make our government not only functional again, but how we can bring about fundamental change that can help revive the middle class.

In the chapters that follow, I will try to help simplify some very complex issues and offer both a solution and a plan that I believe can offer us an opportunity to make our government work for us and help the middle class thrive and grow.

CHAPTER 2 - THE CORRUPTION OF OUR CONGRESS

I said this book is really about the U. S. Congress.   Let me explain why.

Aside from a literal civil war, which I hope no one wants, legislation is the only path I see to solving our plight and Congress makes the laws.

If we go back to the Lake Wealth illustration, Congress is the gatekeeper.   They control which way things flow. They hold the power to divert wealth to the already wealthy or back to the middle class.   Congress is the POTENTIAL solution, but currently, Congress is the biggest problem.

The fact is, our Congress already belongs to the wealthy.

I think you probably already know this, but it is imperative for us to understand why it is currently IMPOSSIBLE for Congress to represent the interests of middle class/ working class Americans.   I am certain that virtually every member of Congress will likely deny that statement vehemently, and swear their undying allegiance to the middle class.   But the facts indicate otherwise.

I would like to add a sidebar here.

It also seems likely that their continued lack of concern for the people who form the backbone of our nation is the underlying because of the anger and angst that has bubbled to the surface in the recent presidential elections.

Let me tell you why I say that.

We have all been raised with the idea that in America we are self-governed, that we get to choose people who will look out for our interests and elect them to govern us. Consequently, we have believed and WANT to believe that we have a government that works for us.   We have been taught that all our lives. Yet, repeatedly and consistently the facts show us that such is NOT the case.   So we become distressed, frustrated and yes, angry.   Not knowing what else to do, we start to turn on each other, pointing fingers, looking for someone to blame and stoking the underlying flames of frustration and resentment to a boiling point.

I believe having such a consistently dysfunctional Congress is a major factor in the divisiveness and acts of disrespect and outright hatred currently on display in our nation.

Congress is not solely responsible for those acts, but their continued refusal to do what they are elected to do is a major contributor and trigger for those behaviors.

Now, back to discussing representation.   I contend that our Congress DOES NOT represent us, and furthermore, I believe it CAN NOT!   It is simply impossible.   Please, let me explain.

I am painting a pretty dismal picture, I know, but consider this: According to the Federal Elections Commission, which monitors campaign revenue and spending for every national election, the average campaign for a seat in the U. S. House of Representatives currently costs over a million and a half dollars per candidate.   The campaign costs for a Senate seat are about seven times that, and considerably more in tightly contested races.

If we are not an incumbent and want to run for a Congressional seat, we will   likely have to start our campaign using our own money.   This means we would have to have tens of thousands, likely hundreds of thousands of dollars in disposable income just to be able to START a campaign for a Congressional seat.   In short, in order to run for a congressional office, we either have to be wealthy and/or be well connected to wealthy friends who will finance our campaign.

Seems to me that pretty well rules out the middle class and we haven't even gotten to the elections.   I mean, how many millionaire friends do those of us in the middle class have?   I know my list of rich friends has exactly ZERO names on it, and I suspect that is true for most of middle-class America.

Recently released data shows that just over half of the Congress sworn in January of 2017 are already millionaires, and virtually no one leaves who is not in the multi-millionaires club!

Excuse my skepticism, but it seems to me that there is just no way that 535 millionaires and about-to-be-millionaires can even begin to understand what it is like to be the average middle-class Joe or Jane in America.   They cannot possibly understand the struggles and the choices we have to make, how hard it can be to come up with several hundred much less several thousand dollars for the unexpected expenses in life, on top of often barely affordable living expenses.   They do not understand the decisions we face and the sacrifices we make to help our children, and often our parents, just get through life.

And there is certainly little to no connection to or understanding for the poor in our Congress.

Let me ask another question.   Why for at least the last forty years, have national approval ratings for our Congress remained been between 10 and 16 percent?   Stated differently, at any given moment, 84-90% of Americans DISAPPROVE of Congress, yet nothing changes.   That fact has bugged me for as long as I can remember. How can a group of people perform so poorly so consistently and keep their jobs?   You or I certainly could not do that.

Well, who exactly are the 10 to 16 percent that is happy with the congressional performance?   The answer simply has to be the people who are profiting from Congress operating the way it does.   So if only 10-16 percent of the country is happy with Congress, but Congress never changes, who really is in control?   It HAS to be the 10-16 percent!   Those would just happen to be the RICHEST 10-16 percent in our country, NOT the rest of us who are the working middle class and the poor.

By the way, it seems more than coincidental that the 13% of the people in our nation who only think minor election reform is needed almost exactly parallels the number of people who think Congress is doing a good job, which would be the same crowd that Congress is making richer.

And THERE is the very heart of the economic warfare, the class warfare that has crept up on us and engulfed us without our even taking notice.   We have not realized it, but it turns out, we only BELIEVE we have a voice in our government.

I realize that sounds cynical, but I am just getting started. As I said, we haven't even gotten to, much less past an election yet and we have already eliminated almost everyone as candidates because those of us in the middle class simply can't afford to even enter the race.

And that is just an itsy-bitsy, teenie-weenie piece of the problem.   Entering an election campaign is just one ingredient in a very complex recipe.   After elections, things really start to look gloomy for the middle class.

Getting elected is the first step.   It takes a lot of money. You have to be rich or nearly so, just to get your foot in the door.

But that is NOTHING compared to the cost of STAYING elected.

And to that end, almost every sitting member of Congress sells their very soul.   The desire to stay elected, to continually be re-elected becomes the central focus of the lives of the men and women who make up our Congress. The congressional obsession becomes, not to serve the people who elected them, but only to do what is necessary to have their constituents elect them again and again.

Remember that statement as we move along.   It plays a key role in why things are so wildly out of control and why the sitting Congress offers no help or hope to the working class Americans who comprise the majority of this nation.

It is also fair to point out some of the reasons members of Congress have to seek re-election.   There are some very strong motivators, and while I don't think the reasons justify their behavior and choices to achieve re-election, the appeal is obvious.

First is the salary: $174,000 a year from day one.   That immediately puts them in the top 1% of wage earners in America, though it actually may not be all that great if you factor in the cost of maintaining a second home in the greater Washington, DC area.   But it still is FAR more than the vast majority of their constituents ever hope to make.

Add to that excellent health care insurance and a very equitable pension/retirement fund that grows with time served (but is not as exorbitant as many think).   Then consider the fact that Congress only actually works just over half as many days annually as those of us in the middle class (plus they get paid their full salary to campaign full-time for themselves in election years), and you have the makings of a pretty good job by middle-class standards. But that is not all by any means.

Additionally, each Congressional member receives a very loosely regulated $3.5 million to $5.5 million annual budget with which they can hire staff and manage the expenses of running their office.   How would you like to have a budget like that with which to manage your business?

Then there are the lobbyists and big corporations who bring their perks, also known as bribes, to the table. These offers can include staggering amounts of money like six figure incomes for spouses to sit on one or several corporate boards (and do little else but sit), benefits to family members, access to halls of corporate power and much more.   And that is just the stuff we know about.

Total all that up, plus the assurance that there is a near 100% probability that when time comes to leave Congress and retire, we will be very wealthy and both we and at least one generation of descendants will be financially secure for the rest of our lives, and there is a pretty strong formula for desiring continual re-election.

That does not even factor in the prestige that comes from the office plus the power and influence holding such an office affords.

It is also easy to see that when someone really, really WANTS to continue to ride that train and understanding how much money it takes, the environment is very ripe for corruption and greed to take over, which is precisely what has happened.

Look at it this way. Let's say we are a supporter and maybe a minor contributor to our Congressman or Senator's campaign.   Another supporter is a MAJOR contributor to the same Congressman or Senator's campaign. Additionally, the other supporter also helps fund supportive organizations like Political Action Committees, which control millions of dollars worth of direct and indirect resources to help our Congressman or Senator get re-elected.   A bill comes up for consideration.   We like the bill and tell our elected official it is a good idea for our business and suggests the Congressman support it. However, the other supporter weighs in on the same bill with a negative response and suggests the Congressman actively oppose it.

Which voter gets the nod?   Do you really think we get a millisecond of consideration?

What if we add TEN of our like-minded friends and ask the Congressman to support the bill?   THEN, the consideration becomes "Which vote will most likely get me re-elected (not just once but repeatedly)?", NOT, "What is best for the people I represent?"

Oh yes, and that is only dealing with SUPPORTERS. How much attention would I get if I said I did not vote for this person? Is there some practical number less than zero? One of my senators does not even bother to acknowledge my letter or contact if I offer an opposing view to what he is doing. The only exception, I believe is if the numbers are absolutely overwhelming against the direction Congressional members choose, and even then, as I have already shown, the will of the majority is resisted and often gets completely ignored.

And the really sad part is that, no matter how good the bill may be or how many people it may help, it is all but certain that our good Congressman will do all he/she can to look after the largest contributors to their re-election. Just follow the money. That is what our Congress does. The evidence seems overwhelming.

I can come up with no other possible explanation for why the will of 73% or 68% or 85% of America gets absolutely ignored.

We all wish it were different, but we all know it is not.

There are even some politicians who are brave enough to publicly admit the obvious, though most do so as they are leaving or have just left office.

Here are just a few. I can only cite "The internet" as the source here because these quotes, and much more, are cited in several places on several sites, so it is difficult to determine where they originated, but I did check the speeches or publications listed and the quotes are accurate.

• "Allowing people and corporate interest groups and others to spend an unlimited amount of unidentified money has enabled certain individuals to swing any and all elections, whether they are congressional, federal, local, state … Unfortunately and rarely are these people having goals which are in line with those of the general public. History well shows that there is a very selfish game that's going on and that our government has largely been put up for sale." – John Dingell, 29-term Democratic congressman from Michigan, in 2014 just before he retired.

• "When some think tank comes up with the legislation and tells you not to fool with it, why are you even a legislator anymore? You just sit there and take votes and you're kind of a feudal serf for folks with a lot of money." — Dale Schultz, 32-year Republican state legislator in Wisconsin and former state Senate Majority Leader, in 2013 before retiring rather than face a primary challenger backed by Americans for Prosperity. Several months later Schultz said: "I firmly believe that we are beginning in this country to look like a Russian-style oligarchy where a couple of dozen billionaires have basically bought the government."

• "I was directly told, 'you want to be chairman of House Administration, you want to continue to be chairman.' They would actually put in writing that you have to raise $150,000. They still do that — Democrats and Republicans. If you want to be on this committee, it can cost you $50,000 or $100,000 — you have to raise that money in most cases." — Bob Ney, a five-term Republican congressman from Ohio and former chairman of the House Administration Committee who pleaded guilty to corruption charges connected to the Jack Abramoff scandal, in 2013.

• "The alliance of money and the interests that it represents, the access that it affords to those who have it at the expense of those who don't, the agenda that it changes or sets by virtue of its power is steadily silencing the voice of the vast majority of Americans … The truth requires that we call the corrosion of money in politics what it is – it is a form of corruption and it muzzles more Americans than it empowers, and it is an imbalance that the world has taught us can only sow the seeds of unrest." Secretary Of State John Kerry, in 2013 farewell speech to the Senate.

• "The millionaire class and the billionaire class increasingly own the political process, and they own the politicians that go to them for money. … We are moving very, very quickly from a democratic society, one person, one vote, to an oligarchic form of society, where billionaires would be determining who the elected officials of this country are." — Sen. Bernie Sanders, I-Vt., in 2015. Sanders has also said many similar things, such as "I think many people have the mistaken impression that Congress regulates Wall Street. … The real truth is that Wall Street regulates the Congress."

• "American democracy has been hacked. … The United States Congress … is now incapable of passing laws without permission from the corporate lobbies and other special interests that control their campaign finances." — Al Gore, former vice president, in his 2013 book The Future.

There's plenty more, but that will suffice.   These are comments from legislators, recent legislators, who actually lived and operated within the system, admitting clearly that Washington is absolutely corrupt.

This is not speculation or some wing-nut conspiracy theory. This is confirmation of facts. Most of us don't even give it a second thought. We have tolerated these levels of corruption for so long, we have begun to look at them both as normal and acceptable.

Hopefully we can agree that it is NEITHER, and that it is time for a change.

I really think we are where we are simply because we don't know what else to do. We know what is going on but we have no idea how to actually change it. Well, please pay attention, because I'm going to explain how we can make it different.

But for now, can we agree that the middle class should not expect any help from the current Congress? It's simple. Our lawmakers are rich and controlled by the interests of the richer! Billionaires control millionaires who control the legal system.

If the middle class is going to survive, let alone thrive again, WE MUST CHANGE THAT! We HAVE to change who is in control of Congress.

Oh yes, and it has to be a lot more than coincidence that in the last forty years with Congress doing its business- as-usual, the wealthiest 10% in our country have gone from controlling about 30% of our nation's wealth to 90%. If we can't look at that and see who is running our government and figure out that where we are headed cannot possibly be good for the middle class, then I'm sorry, but we must simply be brain dead and just haven't quit breathing. And if we think for a minute that the wealthiest 10% in this country, taken as a group, give a damn about us and our middle-class lives, then all I can do is shake my head! We should hold a couple of fingers to our necks and see if our hearts are still pumping blood to our brains.

All of which, and much more, is why I say our current Congress is our biggest problem, and yet presents our ONLY solution to revitalizing our middle class. Congressmen and Congresswomen are rich folks, supported by rich folks, heavily influenced by rich folks, dependent on rich folks to get re-elected and consequently, looking out for rich folks. It seems obvious that our Congress would much rather hang out where 90% of all the wealth in our nation hangs out than the area that shares the remaining 10%.

Once again, just for emphasis, here is my point. Help for the middle class is ONLY going to come from the middle class! If we want to strengthen the middle class, we must make better use of our privilege to vote and looking at the statistics, I'd say we probably need to do so quickly.

So, I have a plan. It's pretty bold and really big. The odds are pretty long, but a hell of a lot better than those offered by sticking with the status quo.

As crazy as it sounds, and I do not mean to sound egotistical at all, but I think my plan may be the ONLY real hope we have of saving, strengthening and expanding the middle class. I say that not because it is my plan, but because I am certain we CAN make it work, and because I simply don't see many other real plans out there at the moment.

Whether it has been intentional or not, we are in a "We" versus "They" economic battle that, if we lose, could mean our extinction as a social class in a generation or two, maybe even an election cycle or two.

But before I explain the details of my plan to you, I have to give you some more bad news.   I want you to be really mad at the status quo before we start talking about solutions.   It's like the movies.   The madder we get at the bad guy character, the more pleasure we get the moment he or she is defeated.

The madder we get at the Congress, the more excited we will be about the solution!

Keep reading...

CHAPTER 3 - IT'S COMPLICATED

I really hate being the bearer of bad news, but there is plenty more, and it is news of which we all need to be aware.

But before that discussion, please bear with me while I explain, for those of us who have forgotten, how laws are created.   I believe we need to have a basic understanding of the process in order to understand both the problem and the proposed solution.

Just as a primer, to help us understand what we are up against, please indulge me while I walk us through an overview of what goes on in Congress.

All laws begin as ideas.   Someone has an idea to create something, fund something, improve something or regulate something that they believe will benefit the citizens of our nation.   That idea comes to or is given to a U.S. Congressman or Congresswoman who then creates a bill proposing the idea for consideration.

According to the official website for the U.S. House of Representatives (www.house.gov), the process goes like this: "Laws begin as ideas.   First, a representative sponsors a bill.   The bill is then assigned to a committee for study.   If released by the committee, the bill is put on a calendar to be voted on, debated or amended.   If the bill passes by a simple majority (218 of 435), the bill moves to the Senate.   In the Senate, the bill is assigned to another committee and, if released, debated and voted on.   Again, a simple majority (51 of 100) passes the bill.   Finally, a conference committee made of House and Senate members works out any differences between the House and Senate versions of the bill. The resulting bill returns to the House and Senate for final approval. The Government Printing Office prints the revised bill in a process called enrolling. The President has 10 days to sign or veto the enrolled bill."

That is a huge over-simplification of what actually happens, but it gets us started and gives us a point of reference as we track this process.

Reading that one paragraph gives us the sense that making laws is a pretty straightforward process, though, right? Assuming that the process worked, there should be a fairly efficient system to consider new legislation and modify or terminate existing legislation as the needs of the public-at-large change.

Well, it was designed to be that way, and it should be. But as we are about to see, IT IS NOT!

There are dozens of ways an excellent idea with exceptional national value can get lost or crushed within the legislative process, which is what usually happens.

Let me explain just a few.

We have already seen that the first problem is that the election process itself severely culls down the candidate pool, which in turn culls down the idea pool. Consequently, Washington has a SEVERE shortage of ideas and spends most of their time infighting and rehashing the same old battles.

But moving past the election process, let's say an elected official has or is given a really wonderful idea. What happens?

Then we look at the bog that becomes a black hole into which almost all really wonderful ideas simply disappear.

While the U.S.House website says a bill then goes to a committee, which is not quite accurate.   The bill will likely go first to a subcommittee, from which it must emerge before it even gets committee consideration.

So what can hold it up? Plenty!

First, there is party fealty . As we will see as we continue, most legislators are far more interested in doing what they are told by their respective parties than they are looking out for what is best for America.

There are in-house rules in both the House of Representatives and the Senate that state that the majority party gets to decide who the chairperson will be in both the committees and the subcommittees.   The chairperson is the person who has the COMPLETE say in what bills will be discussed.

Further complicating things is the overriding mentality throughout Congress being, "regardless of what the other party suggests, it is automatically a bad idea just because it came from the other party."   Then add the acrimonious attitudes the parties have for each other, and you begin to understand this hurdle.   Whether a bill that ever gets out of a subcommittee is dependent solely on which party is in control.

If we need verification of party fealty and how it chokes potentially beneficial legislation, just look at history.   Not much research is necessary to see that Congress has a LONG history of voting strictly along party lines on significant issues.   There have even been several instances in my lifetime where Congress allows partisan gridlock to actually shut down the entire federal government.

This great divide is further polarized by each party's caucus, which is basically time spent with each side meeting separately and the party base mandating to the members of the caucus how each side will oppose the other side's agenda, regardless of whether or not an idea being discussed might benefit the country.   Any break in the ranks will most certainly mean no financial help from the party during re-election campaigns, or even worse that the party will actually fund a competitor's campaign.

Almost no one has the guts to support the other side, even if they agree with them.   To do so amounts to political suicide, and remember, once in Congress, NO ONE wants to leave.

Additionally, we can be assured that between discussion times, lawmakers are on the phone with their major donors getting input and feedback.   No Congressperson wants to risk losing a major financial player over an idea that could be squashed in a subcommittee meeting with almost no public awareness or fallout.

Remember, I told you to hang on to the thought that THE most important objective to every member of Congress is to GET RE-ELECTED?   Well, party fealty is the first place that comes into play.   In order to get elected and/or re-elected, party support is almost a necessity.   Out of 535 sitting members, 435 in the House of Representatives and 100 in the Senate, there are only two members, both Senators, who are neither Democrat nor Republican.   The party is a major source of funding, and funding is necessary for re-election.   Whatever the party heads mandate, the party members support, like it or not.

Want proof?   Just notice, in our recent Presidential election, that all the candidates for the Republican nomination vehemently decried the eventual nominee, and how every single one of them, no matter how strong their aversion to the candidate was during and even after the primaries, ALL eventually "ate crow", and sucked up to the nominee to stay in the party's favor.   Party fealty absolutely reigns supreme, ranking much higher throughout the entire Congress than loyalty to our nation.

This is the "normal" behavior on BOTH sides of the aisle. It does not matter which party has the majority; this is the platform from which they both conduct their business. Congress is deeply divided, extremely polarized on major issues, and absolutely determined to stay that way.   Their idea of compromise is when the other side sees things their way, and we all know the odds of that happening.   We have better odds of winning the lottery without buying a lottery ticket.

And we still haven't even gotten a bill out of a subcommittee yet.

Are we starting to get the picture?   The partisan divide is almost impassable.   Hope for any significant legislation to give any advantage to the middle class is virtually nonexistent.   Congress piddles around the periphery and presents the image of being effective, but we never hear discussion of major issues and things that really must be handled only at the Congressional level.

So far we see that we have an election system that excludes anyone but the very rich from even being a real candidate. The candidates who are elected take office already beholden to their major donors including their political party.   Then we have two deeply divided parties with polar opposite objectives showing absolutely no willingness to compromise on the real issues facing our nation.

Next, we add lobbyists to the mix. Lobbyists are representatives of big companies, big industries and big money who come to Washington to make sure their case is heard by individual Congresspersons.   Usually, they come bearing "gifts" to get lawmakers' attention.   These can be from oil companies, gun companies, drug companies, automobile companies, the medical communities, AARP, or a gigantic hoard of others.

In 2016, there were almost 11,000 lobbyists to whom a collective budget of 2.4 BILLION DOLLARS was paid by their respective interests.   And that is just what is reported.   Any guesses where most of that money went? Well, just for consideration, if you split $2.4 billion dollars 50/50 between the lobbying firms themselves and the various "benefits" they are hired to offer to members of Congress, that averages out to $2,250,000 per Congressperson per year.   I have no proof where all that money went, but it did not vanish into thin air and I'm not stupid.   Even giving everyone as much benefit-of-the-doubt as possible, it still stinks.

The "gifts" the lobbyists bring could be significant campaign pledges through anonymous donors.   They could be lucrative spousal positions on various boards of directors.   They could be a wide variety of "perks" to family members.   They could even be large amounts of cash, but of course, that is not likely the case (ha ha, snicker snicker)... at least so we are told.   (That would be blatantly illegal.)We each have to decide whether we believe it or not.   For those who do, I have some oceanfront property in Arizona that I'll sell you at a bargain basement price.

One thing is certain, every "gift" and every dollar comes with strings attached, and they all are intended to influence the lawmaker.   When the people sending the gifts want something, they call their favorite group of lawmakers in Washington to see that it gets done and guess what, Washington responds!

This is what our newly elected president said on the campaign trail, "I gave to many people, before this, before two months ago [when he officially launched his campaign], I was a businessman.   I give to everybody.   When they call, I give.   And do you know what?   When I need something from them two years later, three years later, I call them, they are there for me.   And that's a broken system."

Seems like a confirmation of the obvious, doesn't it? Money comes calling, and Congressmen and women accept, strings and all.

Yes, we are all humans.   Yes, we are all susceptible to greed, but NO it is not acceptable to take these obvious bribes, and doing so absolutely should NOT be tolerated. Yet we, the voting public, sit back and just accept it as part of the way Washington does business.

I'm pretty sick and tired of it, especially now that I see the process is about to affect the very well-being of my family and me.   I believe it HAS to be changed, and Washington is not going to change it.

So we have large companies and industries actively engaged in spending vast sums of money buying favor and influence with congressional members.   When we add to this equation the personal and self-serving agendas of the members of Congress, we begin to understand that Congress REALLY IS NOT interested in helping the middle class!

There are many more complications, and we will address some of them in the next chapter.   I want us to take a breather and perhaps re-read this chapter.   Like I said earlier, I want us all to be angry.   No, I want us all to be FURIOUS at how broken our system has become and how a government designed to give the citizens of our nation the tools needed to enjoy "life, liberty and the pursuit of happiness" is actually raping the very people for whom it is supposed to provide, and doing it for their own benefit.

I guess I want to give everyone the benefit of the doubt.   I believe that initially, we elect people to Congress who want to make a difference, and there are likely people in our Congress who want change.   However, the deck is so stacked against change that change simply never occurs.

If you have ANY doubt that corruption reigns in Washington, please consider the following: The VERY FIRST act of the Congress that convened in January of 2017 was for the majority party, the Republicans, to call a BEHIND-CLOSED-DOORS SESSION with the SOLE purpose of gutting the House Ethics Committee and making it virtually powerless.   Even though the move was halted temporarily because of public outcry, you can be assured that the issue is not dead and that the intent is still strong to go ahead with the idea. Watch closely. We WILL see it happen. The Ethics Committee WILL be gutted of any authority or ability for Congressional oversight by the current Congress.

What does that tell us about the extent of the corruption on Capitol Hill? It certainly does not indicate any plans to change direction, nor any make any attempt to even hide their corruption!

The net result of all of this is, on an almost daily basis, Congress sells out our future and the future of our children and grandchildren to the highest bidder. They steal opportunity from us so those who already have almost everything can have even more. Is that not a reason to consider doing whatever we have to do in order to change things while we can? Is that not reason around which we ALL can rally to create real change?

Before we can fix it, we are going to have to be extremely motivated to sustain the political will to do what we need to do. Fear and anger are two powerful forces. I hope the fear of losing the middle class and the anger that hopefully exists over all the corruption will combine to allow us to get the job done.

The Washington bureaucracy is deeply entrenched, well funded, and powerfully connected. We have all witnessed every conceivable kind of dirty trick and of taking every possible advantage to continue doing things the way they are currently done. Making real change will not be for the faint-hearted or the uncommitted.

Anger and fear are powerful motivators.

Let me stoke those embers some more... keep reading.

CHAPTER 4 - MURKIER AND MURKIER

We have just seen that the process of making laws is incredibly complex, corrupt and that MANY things being done are not in the interest of the middle class.   But we are not finished. There is more we need to discuss.

Let's go back to the description of the law-making process offered on the U.S. House of Representatives official website.

So far we've seen that there are a lot of obstacles through and around which an idea must pass just to become a bill to even be discussed in a committee.   What happens next?

IF a bill gets discussed/debated in a committee and survives, then it goes to be considered, debated, and/or amended before the entire House of Representatives, where there are continued party acrimony and polarization.

IF a bill clears the entire House then the process starts all over again in the Senate, whose members pride themselves on being even more slow-moving and wrapped up in theatrics and finger-pointing than the House.   First a Senate subcommittee, then a Senate committee, then to the entire Senate.

THEN, if a bill has made it that far and has cleared BOTH legislative chambers, it is sent to ANOTHER committee made up jointly of members of both the House of Representatives and the Senate to iron out any compromises needed.   A bill can come this far and still easily be killed by polarized, hard-line politics or if one or two members of this committee are leaned on heavily by the special interests to which they have indebted themselves.

Therefore, as things currently stand, any bill that passes through Congress to become actual law is a bill that is designed primarily to keep a party's base happy, maintain the party line, satisfy the deep-pocketed contributors, and contribute to the re-election of the voting member, all of which is considered BEFORE anyone even thinks about whether or not it is good for our country.

And if all of that weren't enough, let me describe yet another hurdle. It is called earmarking.

I will explain exactly what earmarking is in just a moment, but I have to discuss a bit of a back story first. I am including this information about earmarking as a preemptive measure, because I am certain that after this is published, it will again become a major factor within the halls of Congress.

As of this writing, earmarking is a practice that has been halted for about the last six years because of public outcry. The issue of earmarking has been used by the Republican Party to help gain control of the House of Representatives, though both parties and both Houses of Congress have a long history or using earmarks regularly.

I have included the subject in my book because now the very same Republican Party who decried earmarking to get control, NOW want to reinstate the practice, to the joy of BOTH parties. Earmarks are about to become a part of our lives again, and is something we should all understand.

Remember I said that for every single member of Congress, the number one, primary, all-consuming goal is to get re-elected over and over again. Well, this is one of their most potent secret weapons used to accomplish that objective.

Earmarks are each Congressional members' "ace-in-the-hole" for re-election. Earmarks are "special projects" that will help only those people whom a congressional member needs in order to be re-elected. Though being elected to Congress is a federal job, we are elected by our respective localized constituencies who are as diverse as the population of our entire country. Local constituents are comprised of all different races and interests and every congressional member has a set of pet projects which are held as bargaining chips when opportunities arise.

An earmark could be a stretch of highway, a bridge, subsidies to a particular industry, grants, special tax consideration for an industry, ANYTHING needed to give them leverage among the local people in a bid for re-election.

While there is nothing inherently wrong with using federal tax dollars to aid some limited local projects, it is the way in which members of Congress use them that is upsetting. They provide members of Congress the ability to hold the entire legislative process hostage, and grind the lawmaking process to a halt, just so they can impose their personal bargaining chip to help get themselves re-elected.

Here is how the earmarking process works. Let's say a bill has made it through the House and goes to the Senate (though earmarking happens in both houses). The bill under consideration is generally popular and beneficial and may even have some bipartisan support. Let's say for example it is a bill to improve veteran's benefits.   No one can seriously object to helping our veterans, right?   We would think it should be a pretty straightforward process to pass the bill, right?

Well, not so fast. Remember that if we land a job in Congress, we view it as a career move.   We come wanting to stay until we retire.   One of the very first things we do as a newly-elected official does is to set up a re-election fund.   We all come to Washington wanting to make Congress our last job change.

In order to do that, we have to get re-elected and to get re-elected, we have to take care of the people who elected us.

So, when this generally popular bill comes through, we are happy to rally to support the bill….. IF AND ONLY IF we can just add our earmark to the bill.   In other words, we refuse to support a bill that could actually benefit thousands of Americans who faithfully serve their nation, unless we get to add the expense of our pet project to aid in our own re-election bid.   Earmarks allow us to go back to the folks that elect us and brag about how hard we have been working for our constituents since we went to Washington.

We actually hold the interests of America-at-large hostage (and think it is OK to do so), refusing to do something good for their country unless we get to add our earmark, our homerun-swing we are saving for just this moment to buy ourselves some "get me re-elected" insurance at the expense of the American taxpayer.

This is what is typically referred to as "pork barrel spending."   It utilizes tax dollars from the entire country for a project that benefits only the citizens of one

Congressional district or state for the sole purpose of getting the sitting Congressional member re-elected.

So, if a bill originally proposed allocating, say, $100 million dollars for something that would actually serve the country, by the time it circulates through Congress and made it to the floor for a vote, it could, and usually does end up costing MUCH more than the original cost and serving mostly to make sure those with the current political power keep it.

About six years ago, the use of earmarks was halted because of public uproar and as a move by the newly elected majority party to show the public that their voices are heard.   Turns out that is more smoke and mirrors.   In every Congressional session since, attempts have been made to quietly revive earmarks, and it looks like this year will be the jackpot.   Interestingly, the move to reinstate earmarks is by the same party who made such a show of halting them.

If it doesn't happen this session, it won't be too long.   They will return and I'll bet it happens in the very near future. They have even been given a new name.   They are now called "Congressionally directed spending."

Both Democrats and Republicans seem to feel that lack of earmarks contributes to even more gridlock, so they are about to revive their use.   Yes, that is correct.   The excuse to bring back earmarks, I mean Congressionally directed spending, is actually that they make government run smoother.   It seems that if there is no political grease, the wheels of government grind to a halt. So much for discussion, fact-gathering,negotiation, and looking out for the interests of the American taxpayer.

In other words, the overriding attitude of every member of our Congress seems to be, "If I can't use my vote to help me get re-elected, then why support a bill?"   What drives legislation in Washington, more than any other factor, is how much re-election fuel laws create.

Sadly, and to the great expense of the average American, this is how Washington operates, has been operating and will continue to operate if we don't change it.   Doing whatever it takes to keep oneself re-elected, first and foremost, is the accepted way to get things done in our Congress.   Based not on the words that come from Congresspersons, but on their actions, it is clear that the real battle cry of Congress is "self-interest above all!"

We, the average, middle-class, hard-working citizens who now have virtually no voice left in Washington, get stuck with the bill, not only for the debacle of creating the law but paying for all the earmarks as well.

All of this information collectively gives us a glimpse of the complexities of the Legislative Branch of our government, but even this description is substantially understated.

As I close this chapter, let's be honest.   We need to take a look at the REAL reason there is no progress in Washington.

It all boils down to this: There is no change in Washington because no one in Washington wants to change. Regardless of which party is in power, both sides really like the way things are going.   The job pays MUCH more money than the most people make.   We have accepted the Congressional behavior as normal for so long that there is no reason to seek change.   The perks are excellent.

Getting rich is fun. So is having the power to govern you and me. Why change?   No one in Congress really wants change, otherwise, things would be changed.

For example, just a few simple changes could dramatically affect our government.   If the House of Representatives passed an internal rule that every spending/funding bill must be debated on its own merit, it would virtually abolish earmarks and the impact of just that one rule changed would save us billions of dollars.   We are not even talking about passing a law, just   simple, in-house rule change in ONE chamber of Congress, would do the trick. No one dares even suggest it.

It would be a very simple matter for the Congress to create laws that would allow for a more inclusive candidate pool and to severely limit the power and impact of the very wealthy and the special interests.   There is just NO way, given the current level of corruption within Congress, that legislation would ever get out of a committee.   To be a committee chairperson means we have been around long enough to be deeply indebted to those who fund our re-elections.   Currently, there is absolutely NO WAY we are going to get the idea EVER discussed of cutting those revenue streams and reducing corporate influence.

Americans have known about these problems and politicians have talked about campaign finance reform for decades.   Yet neither political side nor chamber of the legislature has ever made a serious move to do ANYTHING other than TALK about reforming contribution laws BEFORE an election.   Once elected, Congress continues to enact rules and legislation which result only in ensuring that those in power keep it and that "business as usual" continues in Washington.

If we are waiting for change to come from Washington, we may as well be waiting for the earth to reverse its spin and the sun to rise in the west.

Unforced change is simply NOT HAPPENING!   Why should it?   We have been doing what we do and tolerating what we tolerate for so long no one feels threatened to change. We have given Congress a sense of invincibility.   As a group, I believe we have created the sense that the current behavior in Congress is simply untouchable by allowing this self-serving behavior to just go on and on.

Is it really that bad, we ask?

Well, let's take a known problem. Pick one: Social Security expenses rising faster than current withholding taxes are able to support, immigration reform, growing Medicare/Medicaid costs, the soaring cost of health care, failing infrastructure, job creation, global warming.   It doesn't matter.

Choose one.

We all know these problems and more are out there in plain sight.   We have seen the news for years, sometimes for decades.   We all know these issues need attention. Huge numbers of people, hundreds of millions, are affected. These problems affect every imaginable demographic and conceivable walk of life.   We know no progress will be made without intelligent discussion, serious negotiation and often without serious sacrifice.

Name ONE of these problems on which Congress has made any significant progress in the last year.   How about five years?   Ten?   Is there ANY serious attempt to solve these problems?   If there is, it is likely only to get us past an election cycle or two.   Then things have to be renegotiated.   Congress DOES NOT WANT TO SOLVE PROBLEMS.   Problems are necessary so there are things over which to bicker in the campaign season.   Getting elected to solve problems is much more lucrative than actually solving them.

Imagine trying to successfully navigate complicated, widely beneficial legislation through both houses of Congress with all the ego, corporate money, party fealty, and self-interests overlapping at every turn.   Not to mention any solution is going to involve actual open discussion and willingness to compromise, neither of which seem to even exist in Congress anymore.

Do we see or anticipate solutions in the future?   We WANT solutions, but do we actually see any developing?   None shows up on my political radar.

We have better odds of walking blindfolded through 10 miles of dense forest and not hitting a tree than we have of our current Congress solving big problems.

Yes, it is THAT bad, and getting worse!   And remember, we started this entire discussion because the middle class is in trouble.   The rate of wealth transferring from the middle class to the already rich is faster than it has ever been and is continuing to pick up speed.   The power vested in Congress is the only hope we have for changing things, and the people who hold the power are generally incredibly self-interested and corrupt.

We are simply running out of time!   Something must be done!

So what do we do?

Well, we all know what needs to be done, but I'm saving my answer for a little while yet.

There is more information we need to discuss before I tell you what I have in mind.

Hang in there with me.   We are moving towards an answer and a suggested solution. We will get there soon, I promise.

Keep reading.

CHAPTER 5 - DISASTROUS DELEGATION

If we have managed to get this far and our blood is not boiling with rage, this ought to get us absolutely steaming!

This short chapter is my "aim for the fence" swing.   I hope it connects!

I am pretty sure I can speak for most of us when I say that I am sick and tired of so much government regulation, or phrased more aptly, OVER-REGULATION.

I know that it certainly affects the trucking business and makes it very difficult for those of us in the business to stay in compliance with all the rules and still manage to make a living.   I'm sure it will come as no surprise to you that it gets worse every year.

That certainly is not a problem that is exclusive to the trucking industry.   It is almost universal.

For years I have joked with my kids that "The greatest threat to our democracy is bureaucrats with time on their hands."

Turns out, it's no joke.

It seems to be embedded in the DNA of most bureaucrats to be constantly trying to expand their power and their authority.   They do that by creating an endless stream of more and more rules and regulations.   Bureaucracies left unattended tend to just keep growing . We have certainly come to expect that from Washington, and we have not been disappointed.

The news I'm about to reveal to you is in two parts, so hang on till the end to get the full effect.   If this doesn't make us all so mad we can chew twenty-penny nails and spit staples, then just close my book and go to bed, because if this doesn't get us fired up, nothing else I can say will matter.

First of all, we have allowed Congress to almost completely abdicate their responsibility as lawmakers.   The the day-to-day oversight of our government has been almost completely turned over to a plethora of federal regulatory agencies.   These agencies like the Federal Trade Commission, The Federal Communications Commission, The EPA and many more, with absolutely NO Congressional oversight, have absolutely inundated nearly every business in America with THOUSANDS of bureaucratic rules and regulations.

I am certain you have felt the effects in your business just as I have in mine.

Let me say that I am not an anarchist.   WE NEED RULES AND REGULATIONS.   I believe regulation needs to be done in a responsible manner that considers both one's ability to be profitable AND the needs of the public at large concerning labor practices, environmental concerns and civil rights.

However, what we have currently is incredibly out of control.

In the last four years alone (I got tired of counting, and sick of what I was finding so I only covered four years) these agencies have absolutely smothered us with OVER 10,000 rules and regulations, totaling SEVERAL HUNDRED THOUSAND PAGES of bureaucratic crap, often written and implemented by people who have NO experience in the field they oversee, and have no idea of what it takes to actually run a business in that field.

So, the result is that we have unelected, unmanaged and ill-informed government workers creating policy after policy and rule after rule, with absolutely NO Congressional oversight.   The result is a bureaucratic quagmire and a business owner's nightmare.   This happens because our Congress has not been doing its job and is currently unwilling to do so.   And as we would imagine, the pace is increasing.   2016 set the record for the most rules enacted and the most pages added to the Federal Register, where the end result of all this rule-making is stored.

At the rate we are going, we will have to build a multi-story annex onto the Library of Congress just to have a place to store all the rules and regulations.

Now, that, all by itself, makes my jaw clench and the veins swell in my neck, but that is not all!

Wouldn't we all like to know what Congress does with all the time they save by delegating away all their responsibility?

Well, try not to explode as I explain.   I know it is all I can do to keep my eyes from bulging with rage.

On April 24, 2016, the CBS program, "60 Minutes," interviewed a newly elected U.S. Congressman, Mr. David Jolly, who out of sheer frustration decided to become a Congressional whistle-blower.   We should ALL Google the story and read the original and all of the follow-up stories.

The short version is that when this Congressman went to an orientation regarding his new job responsibilities, he was taken to a room with a whiteboard that had a financial breakdown showing the cost of his re-election campaign which was then broken down into how much money the Congressman needed to raise EACH DAY in order to finance his re-election campaign.

THEN, he was given a schedule that showed that for FOUR HOURS OF EACH WORKDAY, his responsibility was to leave the Capitol Building and walk down the street (because what he was about to do is illegal within his office) and enter what amounts to a telemarketing boiler room where he is to sit on the phone for four hours of the work day and solicit donations for himself and his party.

Each Congressman receives a script, a calling list, and is placed in a room with a phone and a computer.   A bulletin board in the lobby records the success of each Congressman.   Both parties have their separate rooms.

Please don't take my word for it.   Go check out the story.

So, let me summarize.   We are paying $174,000 salary per year, plus millions of dollars a year in perks and benefits, for someone who only works about half as many days as those of us who pay them, and on the actual work days, we are expected to allow our representatives to spend roughly HALF OF THE DAY ON THE PHONE raising money for re-election campaigns.   This allows and promotes even further obstruction and complication in the lawmaking process!   All the while, we have left a completely unmanaged and unrestricted bureaucratic army of unqualified and uninformed minions.   These minions are left to run amok with rulemaking that tries to micromanage every second of every working day for most Americans.

So we have lawmakers on OUR payroll, literally abdicating any legislative activity or responsibility, making it almost impossible for American business to function, and using the work time for which WE are paying, to raise money for a political party!

Is our blood boiling yet?

Hell, in the trucking business it has actually been mandated that we install electronic tracking devices, at our own expense, so that every single second of every day can be monitored.   Big Brother is definitely alive and well.

What a mess!

If that doesn't enrage all of us, we need to just go crawl in our caskets and close the lid because we must be dead!

I feel pretty sure we can all agree that WE NEED TO STOP THIS NONSENSE.

Keep reading and I'll tell you how.

Chapter 6 - The Lethal, Unseen Force

There is one final ingredient I would like to add to the mix before we move on, and it is something that likely gets overlooked, but is a definite factor in Congressional thinking.   We talk a lot about greedy people but not much discussion covers the power and the draw of greed itself.

Greed is an expression of extreme selfishness.

I believe an argument could be made that it is the most destructive force in the universe.

It is something to which we are all susceptible.   None of us are immune to the temptation or tentacles of greed.   But greed can be overpowering, and just as some people are more susceptible to overeating or some other type of addiction than others, so it is with greed.   Add to that the fact that greed is something that is subtle and insidious.   Much like a drug or alcohol addiction, greed can creep up on us and completely possess us before we realize it.

We must understand that greed itself becomes a formidable foe and force with which to contend.

I have seen greed destroy friendships, pit family members viciously against one another, irreparably fracture partnerships and businesses, and if you are a student of history, you know that it is usually greed that ultimately destroys great nations.

I mention it because greed is the only plausible explanation for why those with so much want still more.   Once greed takes hold, it is simply insatiable.   There is no such thing as "enough," and I believe greed has taken control of virtually every person in Congress, and certainly the ultra-rich who manipulate our lawmakers and who are siphoning off the remaining wealth from the middle class.

Greed changes people.   It almost invariably is accompanied by arrogance and a sense of entitlement. Greed makes people have a different worldview and makes basic changes to virtually everything they think.   When greed takes control, actions once considered unconscionable, suddenly become not only acceptable   but part of an entitlement which we perceive as deserved. When we become greedy, we simply are not the people we once were.   We become aggressively and viciously self-serving.

Greed has many of the characteristics of addiction.   Like most addictions, if we are addicted, we deny there is a problem when the fact is the problem has become uncontrollable.

I'm no preacher, but I know the Bible says greed, that is, the love of money, is the root of all kinds of evil.   It also says we cannot serve God and money, meaning we cannot serve God and be greedy.   It is also one of a short list of characteristics which the Bible specifically states that God hates.

That is enough evidence for me.

If you are of a different faith, I believe the holy writings of every major religion include the same principles and warnings.

There are lots of reasons greed is called one of the seven deadly sins!

In short, it is impossible for greed to accomplish good. IMPOSSIBLE.   Greed forces people to ONLY be self-serving and self-invested.   The interests of the greedy are exactly the opposite of the stated goals of the Constitution to which every Congressional member pledges allegiance.

If we look carefully at our Congress and the people who control our Congress, the hold greed has on our lawmakers manifests itself at every level.   We have millionaires who fill the seats of our Congress and every one of them wants to be re-elected in a quest for more.   That shows they are controlled by greed.   That may not have been the case before being elected, but we can clearly see by the lengths to which members of Congress go seeking re-election, that GREED IS ALIVE AND THRIVING in Congress.

The billionaires who tell the millionaires in our Congress what to do are unquestionably greedy.   When greed besets us, it develops a tight hold on every thought and the mental process we have. Greed obsesses us with thoughts of acquiring more money and power.

And once greed is in control, we are simply no longer the rational people we once may have been.   Suddenly no matter how much we have, it is, and never will be enough.

I've said all that, not to excuse the behaviors of the members of Congress, but to help us understand that it is very likely that people who occupy the seats of Congress are not really the people who were originally elected by their constituents.   If greed is in control of us, we are not in control of ourselves.   It is exactly the same as if an alcoholic takes a drink or a drug addict takes a hit of their drug of choice. Greed turns us into the greedy version of who we once were. If that is the case, it merely reinforces everything I have said about the urgency of doing something about saving the middle class while we still can.

It also reinforces the argument that no help is coming from Washington, and if we want to change, we have to make it happen.

I don't believe that that the rich or the uber-rich are intentionally out to destroy the middle class, but the fact that they are doing so is lost in their pursuit of their ultimate quest... to have even more than they already possess.

Having a Congress that is controlled by greed may explain why even though every Congressman swears an oath to uphold the Constitution and provide for our general welfare, that that oath is subsequently abandoned in the quest to be continually re-elected.

I sincerely hope that this observation will help create urgency in finding a solution to our problems with our Congress.

Greed is a merciless taskmaster. If we don't make changes and quickly, I am afraid all of us may be forced to serve those who are driven by greed.

Chapter 7 - The Three Word Solution

Ok.   We are almost ready for the big reveal... a plan to make Washington work again.

But before we jump into the details of my plan, we have to have a little chat.

I'd like to remind all of us that the government we have, with all its warts and problems, is still OUR government. Believe it or not, Congress works for US.   Well, at least they are on our payroll. Like it or not, they are OUR Congress.

So, if things are rotten in Congress, and I believe they are, it is because WE HAVE ALLOWED THEM TO GET THAT WAY. In fact, we the citizens, as a group, have created this 535-headed monster.

We have allowed, even encouraged the parties to polarize. We have continued to re-elect the same people cycle after cycle.   We should not be surprised that when we keep doing what we are doing, we keep getting more of what we are getting.

As my son is fond of telling me, "That ain't rocket surgery!"

Congressional approval ratings have been between 10 and 16 percent for as long as I can remember.   I know I have been pondering how to rectify that for at least two decades.

The group that approves of Congressional behavior can ONLY be made up of those who elect each individual

Congressman and those who are benefiting (likely profiting) from our Congressman's actions.

I see no other way this re-election trend could continue.

I would just like to point out that every time we re-elect the same people to Congress,we are saying that we are perfectly happy with EVERYTHING that goes on in Congress.   If we keep doing what we are doing, i.e. re-electing the SAME CROWD, then we keep getting what we are getting.   It is absolutely insane to think otherwise!

We may not think our favorite representative is part of the problem, but EVERYONE in Washington is part of the problem.   The system is badly broken and to continue to vote for any part of the status quo, to continue to support anyone that is part of the current system, contributes to the continuation of what is going on.

So, to the people who repeatedly elect our representatives just for their own self-interests, I would like to offer a couple of thoughts to consider.

It's simple really. If we are going to make government work for all of us, we have to go back and heed the powerful words of President John F. Kennedy, now indelibly and irrevocably etched in our history, when he said simply, "Ask not what your country can do for you - ask what you can do for your country."

It is time for us to do for our country.   We created this mess.   We need to clean it up.

Our country NEEDS a strong, dynamic, vibrant middle class. Otherwise, it becomes just another country of rich and poor.

In order to have that, we have to be bigger than political parties.   We have to have and cling to ideas that bring us together, not tear us apart.   If we want to change Washington, we MUST lay down our political party banners and take up American flags.   We MUST set aside our self-interests and pursue the common good. Each and every one of us MUST put America before self.

We must see that what is good for America is good for all of us.   Otherwise, we kill the goose that lays the golden eggs. If we eliminate the middle class, then we drive a stake through the heart of America.

If we have a thriving economy, it is better for the rich AND the poor.   If we fix our health care system, every individual and business benefits.   If we actually have a government that is OF, BY and FOR the people, everyone benefits. It is so obvious and so simple.   We are ALL better if we work together.   We have to stop letting our individual agendas and little pet issues blind us to that fact.

Many of us read a Chinese fable when we were children about a wise man giving a bundle of sticks to a student and telling him to break the sticks.   As long as the sticks were bundled together, they could not be broken.   In order to break the sticks, they had to be taken from the bundle and broken separately.   United we stand.   Divided we fall. The lesson is as old as time itself.

If we keep ourselves fragmented by partisan politics and individual peeves, then we will not win this class war.   We will only be able to salvage the middle class if we work together.

If we are to survive, I believe we must set aside the prospect of scoring any single political victory and fix our Congress so that it can function properly and do what is best for our entire nation.

If we are able to set aside selfish interests, at least for a season, an election cycle or two, we can reclaim our government and make it work for all of us again.   If we are unwilling to do that, then what we repeatedly see and are coming to despise in Washington will continue to grow and fester.   We then resign ourselves to whatever fate those in power determine for us.   We have repeatedly been shown that Congress is far more self-interested than interested in what is good for our nation.   If we don't rise to the task, if we continue down the paths we are headed, I am absolutely positive that most of us will NOT like the destination whenever we arrive.

Our government is currently run by two self-interested extreme viewpoints which are polarized against each other. Party interests far outweigh the interest in doing what is best for our country.

My plan is a way for us, the majority in the middle, who are tired of the fighting, the jockeying for party advantage, the finger-pointing, the unmitigated greed and the childish stubbornness that has gotten us where we are, to work together to make our government work for the good of all of us.

So, having stated my preamble, let's go to my plan.

We have all seen that sending in a few, even a lot of new faces into the Congress in any election cycle simply does not work.   All of our   current options for candidates are likely already a Republican or a Democrat, which means we continue to be subjected to party fealty above national interests. This leaves us right back where we started.

Furthermore, because of the seniority system and the existing House and Senate rules, newbies have virtually no impact on the way things get done.   The rules relegate new members to the least important tasks and are put on committees that where most of the agenda is already decided.

Additionally, we know the problems are longstanding and deeply rooted.   The longer we serve in Congress, the more indebted to the deep pockets we become.   This means we become continually less likely to promote or produce any help for the middle class.

So we know that a very significant changeover, even one that is record-setting, will not solve any problems.   The new energy and ideas brought by the newly elected will just be drained by the system and sucked into the political black hole that Congress now represents.

Based on current behavior and continuing inability to deal with pressing issues, it seems quite evident that, almost to the person, every sitting member of Congress, whether in the House or the Senate, has put their priorities in the following order:

First, plan to get re-elected. An overwhelming desire to be re-elected makes our first priority, of necessity, personal ambition, and greed. We simply MUST do whatever it takes to be re-elected

Second, and closely related to the first, is we need to hold the party line.   We have to keep the party bosses happy so the party will help with our re-election.   Only two people out of 535 are not affiliated with a major party.   Those are pretty long odds. We definitely don't want to have to pay for our own re-election bid.

Third, and also closely related to the desire to get re-elected, we have to keep the deep-pocketed individuals and corporations who fund our campaigns happy.   We certainly want to keep them around both for the re-election funding and for the perks.

Fourth, it is imperative that we keep the people who elected us happy.   We have to serve this group as fully as the previous three priorities will allow.

Finally, last and most definitely least, if our vote happens to benefit the American people at large, well, that would be good.   Absolutely not necessary, mind you, but certainly OK.

Yes, that is a cynical description.   Is there any better explanation for why Congress is consistently and perpetually so ineffectual?   Is there some other reason why longstanding problems continually get overlooked or ignored?

So, I believe with all my heart that there is ONLY ONE WAY to make things work in Washington to benefit the middle class.

Want to hear it?

Its three simple words and they are not "I Love You."

The solution to the problems with Washington lies in the three words: FIRE THEM ALL!

That's right, FIRE EVERY DAMN ONE OF THEM!   Send them packing!

Wow!   Everyone is standing and applauding!   What an idea!

Congress has repeatedly had chance after chance to self-correct and serve the people we have hired by election to serve.   Again and again and again we are disappointed and very unhappy with our choices, at least 84%-90% of us are. As a group, we employ a bunch of self-serving parasites who care about little but themselves.   ENOUGH! OUT WITH THEM! Time for ALL of them to go.

Then we need to replace them with honest, hard-working members of our MIDDLE CLASS; People who understand our world and who will create laws that benefit as many people as possible instead of JUST the rich.

If we want to save and grow our middle class, I believe we absolutely MUST take back our Congress, quickly and decisively by the widest possible margins, and then make it as difficult for the wealthy and the special interests to regain a foothold as we possibly can.

I feel sure there are good, well-intentioned people in our Congress who just can't fix the system.   But, if we REALLY want to change things in Washington, and especially in a short time frame, I believe the circumstances I've just described leave us no option but to clean house... send EVERY sitting member of the House and the Senate packing and start with a clean slate of people who want only to solve some of the problems we face and make our government more functional.

That is the only way to defeat the choke holds of the two parties and all the special interests to which Congress caters. They simply ALL must go! Otherwise, the whole exercise is one of futility.

By the way, that includes the Senators who don't come up for re-election in any given 2-year cycle. Boot them out when their election cycle comes up. They have been part of the problem, too. Why should they be rewarded by being allowed to hang around?

Another crucial benefit of sweeping every available seat in one election would be that we would then have enough representation that we could potentially override even a Presidential veto, should one occur, and the will of the people would finally prevail.

Technically, a complete house-cleaning can't be done in less than six years, but if we swept every available seat in one cycle, or anywhere close, I don't think the remaining Senators could mount enough opposition to stop the momentum. Given that kind of mandate, most probably would not want to. Remaining members, after all, still want to be re-elected.

Most people that I talk to love that concept. I can make a roomful of strangers clap and shout out loud just by suggesting that we "fire them all." I have suggested it to groups of total strangers for years and I HAVE NEVER heard any opposition to the idea. People love it. But if I ask them how we might do that, they are pretty baffled. They love the idea but are really clueless as to how to actually go about it. I mean, we only vote for representatives from our respective districts and states, right?   How can that limited voting ability change anything?

I am going to share a plan that I've pondered for decades, that will allow us to basically restart our government with two rooms full of people who have no special interest connections, no aspirations to become career Congressional members, answer to no political party bosses and whose sole intent in taking their respective offices is to serve the American people and get things back on track to provide for the general welfare and the common interests of our country.

And as an added bonus, if we are busy focused on working toward the things we all want, we will simply not have time or interest in dwelling on whatever differences we may have and things that tear us apart.   We grow more united by and through our efforts.   I think more unity is something America could certainly use a good dose of right now.

Sound too good to be true?

Well, I admit it is a long shot, but it can be done and I'll not only explain how but give you a detailed plan!

Are you ready?

Well, you have to wait for one more chapter.   There is a matter of extreme urgency that we have to discuss first to lay a foundation for our plan.

CHAPTER 8 - DANGEROUS DEBT MENTALITY

I believe I would be remiss in discussing the election of a whole new Congress if I did not share some basic information about our National Debt. This also shows one final example, why this whole idea is so important. This explanation also adds further reinforcement to the idea that our existing Congress is primarily motivated by their own self-interests, as have been a long line of predecessors.

The national debt is "the elephant in the room" in Congress, and it's about as big as the state of Alaska (which if you don't know is bigger than Texas and California combined). Almost NO ONE in Congress will even mention it, much less get it out on the floor and talk about it.

But if we are going to make a serious attempt to solve real financial issues, we certainly need to address this issue and at least possess a basic understanding of the problems this debt creates.

I am bringing it up here because the present Congress absolutely will not. If WE don't address it outside of Congress, just as if WE don't take it on ourselves to bring about change, then it just won't happen.

Year after year the Congressional Budget Office (CBO) and the Government Accountability Office (GAO) warn Congress and the public that what we are doing is simply unsustainable and will lead to insolvency.

Year after year their warnings fall on deaf ears.

Interestingly enough, throughout the incredibly ugly 2016 Presidential campaign, neither side made it an issue, yet it may be the biggest, most important single problem facing future generations in our nation.

The national debt is the aggregate total of all the public debt the federal government has outstanding to date.

Every year Congress and the President negotiate a budget. That budget indicates the plan by which our government will spend the revenue (taxes) they collect from us.   It in no way assures that the plan will be followed, only that we have a track on which to run.

As the year progresses, if they overspend the anticipated revenue, they borrow the difference from the U.S. Treasury. This keeps the government functioning smoothly.

The amount borrowed in any one year is called the "deficit" for that year.

The cumulative total of all of the unpaid yearly deficits is the national debt.   The actual total now increases substantially by the minute, but currently is around $20,000,000,000,000 - yes that is $20 TRILLION dollars.   A trillion is a thousand billion and a billion is a thousand million.   I cannot wrap my head around twenty trillion dollars. We could probably buy a continent for that much money.

Setting aside the unfathomable size, there are still problems that need addressing.   The national debt is fast approaching seven times our national "income," meaning total federal tax revenue, and in fact, may have surpassed that benchmark by the time you read this.

Well, if we go to a bank to borrow money for personal use and we are already seven times our annual household income in debt, I doubt we will be able to get any loan except perhaps a mortgage using property as collateral, and even that would be doubtful.

I know there are differences, but, just as a point of reference, that fact alone should at least trigger caution flags.

Even if, as huge as it is, that sum is really manageable, there are two very closely related and very imposing problems related directly to the debt load that simply MUST be addressed.

One is that we are currently spending over 6% of our national income, that is, all the revenue (taxes) the federal government collects, JUST to pay the interest on all this debt.   That is about $290,000,000,000 (that is 290 BILLION DOLLARS!) a year in interest payments alone that is no longer available for services and programs that benefit our citizens.

Just for the sake of comparison, that is about one-third of our entire military spending budget.

The second and more alarming problem is that there is absolutely no end in sight.   If we listen to government budget plans every year, we ALWAYS hear government officials talk about "deficit spending."   It is now just part of the regular budgeting process. In other words, Congress and the President PLAN, EVERY YEAR, to spend more than we take in.

Now, having the government borrow money can be a good thing.   President Franklin Roosevelt used the idea to rebuild the American economy after the Great Depression. If the government is borrowing with a plan to repay, then debt can be good. Debt repayment usually comes from expanding the economy, meaning more jobs and higher wages, which then creates more tax revenue.

In terms most of us can understand, debt with a plan to repay would be akin to a business loan to a small business person. The intent would be to use the debt to enlarge the business and take in more revenue. This would just be on a federal government scale.

But to PLAN in advance to continue to endlessly borrow with no plan for repayment even being discussed seems not only extremely reckless but ultimately a plan for financial calamity and disaster. And because of all of the problems we've already discussed, any change seems unlikely... no, more like impossible.

Given the new President's cabinet picks and policy announcements to date, and the fact that the Republicans now have a majority in both houses, we will no doubt see unprecedented tax cuts, which will not really be tax cuts at all, but tax deferments.

What do I mean? Well, a tax cut may not really be a tax cut, just a sneaky way for the rich to get richer at our expense.

Let me explain what I mean.

Let me show you when a tax cut is NOT a tax cut at all.

A budget is a plan to disperse revenue. Whether it is a household budget or a budget for an entire nation, the principles are the same. You have income, and you have outgo; revenue, and expenses, and you want the numbers to AT LEAST match.   If the income exceeds the outgo, you have discretionary income to spend or save.   If the outgo exceeds the income, you have a deficit or debt.

In the case of a deficit, to balance the budget, you either have to generate more income (which for the government means increase taxes), make your budget leaner, which means giving up something and in this case it would be benefits to citizens, or you have to tap a credit card or line of credit and go into debt to cover the deficit.   Pretty simple, right?

So when Congress passes a tax cut that hugely reduces revenue and they do not match it with spending cuts, they create more deficit spending and add to the national debt. Republicans will NOT be able to match the pending revenue loss with spending cuts because to do so would eliminate so many benefits from people who need them so badly, they would make people mad enough to elect someone else. Remember they desperately WANT to be re-elected.

They will make some budget cuts as part of a smoke and mirrors routine designed to convince voters that Congress is saving them money, while the resulting difference between income and outgo will be quietly borrowed and is then essentially transferred to the already burgeoning debt load to be dealt with by our children, grandchildren and beyond.

Therefore the "tax cut" will reduce government revenue because the government depends on taxes to operate. Being unable to match the income loss with cuts in benefits, the government borrows the difference (again) and passes along their overspending to future generations.   Today's crowd enjoys more wealth.   Tomorrow's crowd inherits more reckless debt, plus interest.

This practice has become a planned, intentional, ongoing part of the federal government's budgeting process.

So what gets accomplished by a tax cut is that the wealthy become wealthier at the expense of ours and future generations.   Also, the politicians come off looking like heroes to their voters so they can get re-elected, and we, the working class get stuck with the bill and have to clean up the mess down the road.   All the while, we continue a march to economic insolvency and disaster.

You see, Congress does not want to discuss this because those discussions are going to have to include sacrifice, more government revenue (taxes) and fewer benefits, and those are not topics that get them re-elected.   No one wants to talk about more taxes.   No one receiving benefits wants to have to face fewer benefits.   Not popular topics. Not much ground for re-election promises.

PLUS, no one in Congress wants to talk about the national debt because BOTH parties, albeit for different reasons, plan to continue with their habit of deficit spending.   The Democrats want to keep paying for programs without raising the necessary taxes and the Republicans want to cut taxes, and cannot match the revenue loss with expense reductions.

Oh, they will make some token spending cuts which will be painful to the people who are the beneficiaries of the benefits being cut, but it is just another re-election ploy.   It hides facts and gives the voters the impression that they are saving them money simply to garner re-election votes.

What is actually happening, though, is they are trading our economic future and the future of our descendants for their own re-election campaigns.

This is a classic example of Congress making a decision that is good for politicians and a political party, but shows little regard for the American public and our long-term welfare.

So Congress, for at least my generation, has just ignored the issue and pretended it does not exist, proving once again that they lack the courage and honesty to face pressing issues and tell voters the truth about our financial predicament.   Consequently, we keep re-electing a Congress with a severe and perpetual shortage of ideas who continue to demonstrate being selfish and self-serving to the core.   This proves yet again that Congress cares far more about being re-elected than serving our nation.

I believe the old saying is true, "If our outgo continues to exceed our income, then our upkeep will be our downfall."

That isn't rocket surgery, either!

Now it's scary to even think about what would happen if the government should reach a point where a decision is made to just not pay our debts, but given our new President's penchant for declaring bankruptcy, it is certainly a VERY SCARY possibility.   Another option that is at least as scary is to think about what happens to future generations if we don't stop this "it's ok to just keep overspending" mentality.   We need to start talking about solutions and reversing the trend, or when the hurt comes, it is REALLY going to hurt!

If we want to solve some of this mess, if we want to make our government functional again, if we really want our government to be of, by and for the people, it's simple...WE HAVE TO CLEAR THE HOUSE AND GET RID OF EVERY LAST MEMBER OF CONGRESS!   There is just no other way to make any real progress.

Now let me show you exactly how we can do that.   Turn the page...

CHAPTER 9 - AMERICA BEFORE SELF

Well, we have covered the "why" and the "what." Now let's talk about the "how."

How do we change the largest, richest, most deeply entrenched and likely the most resistant-to-change bureaucracy in history in one election cycle? Well, it certainly won't be easy, but it CAN be done if we hurry.

So here's my idea.

I'm calling this a middle class revolution because we need a revolution among voters. We must take our fight to the ballot box, and then we have to win. In order to do that, we have to have our middle class show up at the 2020 voting booths and be solidly united in our purpose and actions.

Can we do that? We can if we stay focused on our goal and vote for America's best interests, not just our own.

Convincing the tens of millions of voters we will need on our side to make this work is a bigger than a gargantuan task, so it will not happen quickly. We have to convince people to vote differently than they typically do. That will be a real challenge. It will have to be done in phases, and a good foundation built on each phase to support the next one which is why I beleive 2020 is the earliest possible date we can make this happen.

The framers of our Constitution made it impossible to completely replace Congress in one election cycle. While the entire House of Representatives is up for re-election at the end of their two-year term, only one-third of the Senate seats are up for election in any given two-year cycle. Senators serve for six-year terms, so only one-third of them are elected every two years.

So the maximum number of Congressional seats available in any two-year election year   is 468, 435 in the House and 33 in the Senate.   There is actually one cycle in every six years where the 100th Senate seat is up for re-election, making the possible seats available in that election year 469.

As I've said, the 2020 election cycle is the absolute soonest I can envision this coming together, and in that cycle, the number of seats available for election in the U. S. Congress is 468.   So giving pink slips to 468 members of our Congress and replacing them with the people we want, all in the 2020 election cycle, is our goal for the Middle Class Revolution.

My goal is to make that year's presidential election the second most-talked about issue on the news and the possibility of electing an (almost) entirely new Congress the lead story.

But things do not stop there.   Electing an entire Congress is complicated AND just a changing of the guard will not necessarily change anything.   We have to elect a Congress that is committed to a mission, OUR mission, the one we must specifically state for this plan to work.

Please allow me to explain.

I've been pondering how to make this happen for well over two decades.   Think about it. The American public has known at some level that Washington is corrupt that entire time, and nothing has changed.

In that time, there have been numerous news stories to substantiate severe government corruption in Washington, and mine is certainly not the first book to be written heralding the plight of the middle class.   Still there has been no change.

So I don't think just writing a book and publicizing what everyone already knows is enough to motivate people to do what we need to do to create change. It hasn't so far.

I think to make this work, we have to do things differently. Instead of electing members to Congress and waiting for them to give us new laws, we have to create the laws we want and need, then find candidates who will commit to the package we put together and elect them all at one time.

There is no single issue that I can think of that would provide the necessary energy and about which middle-class America would rally, so we need an aggregate of ideas to unite us

The way I think we have to do this is to give a broad spectrum of the middle class enough reasons to want change and enough motivation to get them to the polls to vote for change.   The ONLY way I see this ever happening is as a package deal.

The package will no doubt, have some good news and some bad news for almost everyone.   The final package will be a series of trade-offs that, overall, made enough people happy to garner votes for the entire package.   The challenge will be to make the good outweigh the bad for large enough segments of the middle class to actually produce change. It's a "spoonful of sugar helps the medicine go down" kind of plan.

We will have to find enough political hot-buttons and offer enough solutions to those issues to excite the voters. We have to create a political tsunami. And I think we have to do it in ONE swipe, one election cycle, while Capitol Hill is convinced it cannot be done.

Let's surprise and shock the status quo!

Toward that end, we must carefully knit together legislation we, the middle class, want to be passed, and in that legislation deliver enough benefits to enough people that they will show up at the polls on election day determined to "pink slip" the entire Congress , then vote for our candidates because of our promised agenda.

For example, I am a truck driver. I can tell you without a doubt that I know a way to get millions of truck drivers to come vote for our agenda. The needed legislation would not be of interest to most people, but it would sure excite a few million truckers. All we would have to do is just stop the feds from over-regulating the trucking industry, and promise to eliminate some of the unnecessary bureaucratic crap with which we have to contend.

I am sure that is true for dozens of other groups.

Another example might be if we promise our workforce that we will raise the minimum wage and give them specifics. That will attract everyone currently making below the proposed minimum wage. Plus, remember that majority of Americans, 68% according to recent polls, already want the minimum wage raised to $10/ hr. Surely, this promise will attract those voters and give our cause a boost.

If we promise food servers, who currently make a federal minimum wage of $2.13/ hr (slave wages, pure and simple, and utterly shameful), and who have not gotten a raise in over 25 years, that we will double or even triple the minimum wage for servers and bartenders, MILLIONS of them will turn out to vote and will support our candidates and our agenda, almost regardless of what else was on the ballot.

If we promise small business owners REAL assistance to grow their businesses; relief from government over-regulation, access to working capital, assistance with growth planning, employment incentives, etc., and spell out for them in advance of the election EXACTLY what we were promising, I believe millions of them will come out to support us.

If we promise everyone who really cares about integrity and transparency in government that we will reinstate those qualities, and put a plan in writing to do so, I believe a large contingent of the public would welcome and rush to make the needed changes.

Do you get the idea?

I do not have a clue what the final package may include or look like, but in order to get voters to the polls to support us, we must form a coalition of high-value middle-class interests and craft specific legislation which address those concerns.   We will essentially form one gigantic "special interest group" with that interest being to serve the most Americans possible.   We will have every candidate pledge, swear on video that is posted online, and sign a written pledge, to faithfully support the ENTIRE package we have put together, word for word.   For everyone involved, we will have to be "all in," all or nothing.

I believe, in this process, we will have to negotiate the balance of revenue and spending for ourselves and put together a plausible federal budget, demonstrating that balancing a federal budget is possible and that we are committed to doing so.

We will have to suggest ideas, modify them, respectfully debate them, and reach consensus.   We will need to gather information from every demographic of our nation, young, old, rich, poor, every ethnicity... everyone willing to participate, and negotiate and craft ideas that work the best for everyone.   We will all have to be willing to both negotiate and sacrifice if needed, but do all we can to minimize the pain and maximize the benefits for everyone.

That certainly is NOT what is happening in Congress today.

We will basically do what we are paying Congress to do that is not getting done, NOR WILL IT EVER if we don't change it.

However, we will be doing this without input from special interests or big political contributors, political parties or people whose primary interest is their own re-election. We will be designing our package with the focus and priority of doing what is best for our nation and serving the most people possible.   We will not be concerned with making a political party or any particular interest groups happy.   In fact, I am confident that if we do this properly, we will absolutely enrage a LOT of party loyalists as well as the current crop of special interest groups who currently have our current Congress so tightly in their grasp.

Oh well :) There are worse goals we could have!

It seems obvious to me that one primary area of focus in improving the middle class would be to create JOBS, lots and lots of GOOD PAYING jobs; not minimum wage jobs but jobs which will support the needs of American families. Preferably these will be jobs that cannot be exported. Good jobs allow people to have choices and have spendable as well as investable income, expanding the overall economy. We will need to look at and give government support to ideas that foster job creation like making start-up and growth capital for SMALL businesses accessible and affordable.   Education and skills training are also necessary, so it follows that making education and skills training affordable will be part of the package.

Providing sustainable health care solutions that will be accessible to everyone will certainly be welcomed in the discussions.   It is hard to work if we aren't healthy.

We must assure that EVERY American citizen has the unfettered ability to exercise their vote.

I believe another way to grow the middle class is to commit to eliminating poverty and helping poor people become self-sufficient middle-class citizens.   Helping people move from being poor and having very few options to being able to sustain a reasonable middle-class lifestyle is good for everyone.   More people with more disposable income equals more goods and services being sold, which is what makes our economy grow. Less poverty means less burden on the government, not to mention less of the crime that breeds in poverty as really poor people struggle to survive.

I believe that lifting people up is always better than beating people down.

It also seems to me that these are not the values that belong to political parties, but to EVERY AMERICAN. We need ideas that are not separated by a political divide, but ideas that include and value EVERY American.

If you view America's total wealth as a pie chart, my hope and intent is to help middle-class Americans have more "pie." One way to do that is to make the "pie" bigger, so one of the major areas of focus that I hope everyone will embrace is to simply give the poor and the middle class the tools they need to increase the wealth on our side of the great wealth divide.

Once we craft these ideas we combine them into ONE package, and we all must agree to support the entire package even though there will undoubtedly be parts of it that we don't necessarily like. Keep things simple. We will give voters a clear, well-defined choice: If we really want change, vote yes and create the change we have carefully described. Otherwise, vote no and keep getting what we are getting.

Plus, as I've mentioned, this entire project will also have the terrific added advantage of allowing us to all work together on a project with common goals which will help heal and bridge the great political divide that now exists.

It certainly is no secret that our nation faces some severe financial issues, as well as a plethora of other problems. In attempting to solve those problems, no solution is going to make everyone happy. We will all have to have to make sacrifices to rectify the problems.

In other words, our being willing to put America's interests above our own is the ONLY path to change.

We are not stupid.   We understand that these changes likely will mean a large majority of us are choosing to pay more taxes are likely to receive fewer benefits.   We understand that if we raise wages, we also face modest price increases for goods and services. But if we make it clear that our objective is to actually create as much long-term sustainable benefit to everyone as possible, then I believe, we can make it work, especially when the alternative is a middle-class nightmare.

And the fact is, even though we all know there are huge financial problems and solving them would not be fun, Congress is historically unwilling to take on the responsibility for solving real problems because they know that whatever solutions are proposed, they don't offer a lot of re-election material.   We all know that problems don't typically solve themselves, they just continue to grow until something unwanted and for which we are unprepared, breaks down completely.

In our newly-created "do what is best for America" environment, we can put any and all problems on the table for discussion and look at options for solving them, though I am sure there will be times when we don't like ANY of the options.   New ideas will definitely be welcomed and encouraged.

I believe that in this environment, we can do what Congress cannot, that we can work among ourselves and find plausible, real, workable solutions for large and pressing problems.   We can discuss balancing our budget, fixing Social Security, solving immigration issues, and creating legislation that will benefit and grow our middle class. And we can completely block out the corporate and special interests that so far have managed to prevent those efforts.

It is an easy thing to get everyone in a room to agree we should "Fire them all!   Throw out every single one." I know because I've done it for years.   Everyone likes the idea on the surface.   But when people step into the voting booth, they have to have a strong belief that, if they vote for change, what they are getting is better than what they now have. Otherwise, no change will occur.

My goal for this project is to find and develop ideas that are so powerful they will motivate the citizens of our great land to sweep those 468 seats.

It doesn't cost any more to dream big. We may as well go for the whole enchilada.

These will be ideas we develop together and around which we can rally.   Many of these ideas will likely be ideas largely dismissed by Congress, but important to the electorate.   They will have to be ideas that are so much better than the status quo that people will be happy to embrace them.   We will structure and support ideas that serve the best interests of our entire nation, not just a select few.

Following are just a few of the ideas that I believe are necessary to make this happen.

It seems to me that we will certainly want Congressional members held to a much higher standard of ethics than they currently are.   We will also want to demand that the influence of special interests and lobbyists be severely and immediately restricted.

I believe balancing the national budget should be a central objective, though it will not be accomplished in the short term.   At the very least we need a plan to achieve financial balance, and those details will have to be worked out in our proposals.   This will be an incredibly difficult task without any interference from special interests, and is an absolute impossibility if those interests are factored into the equation.

We also need to assure through federal law, that EVERY citizen of this nation has the right AND the unrestricted ability to cast their vote.

I further believe we should commit to an agenda that fosters the growth and revitalization of our middle class.

So, phase one will involve us crafting the package of legislation that would generate enough interest, excitement, ideas and real discussion to make this whole thing work.   Though that task is a formidable task, it is one we can and must do if we want to revitalize the middle class, not to mention salvaging our government and preserving our way of life.

Then phase two will be to find potential candidates in every congressional district in the nation who will pledge to fully support the entire package, convince them to run for the office, support them, fund their campaign and do everything we possibly can to elect them to office in one election cycle.   Show Congress and the world that we have had enough pettiness and crap.   We are sick of greed and total disdain for working class people.   We refuse to continue to elect people to represent us, only to be ignored after the election is over.   We need to say with our votes, loudly and clearly, that the services of the current Congress are no longer wanted or needed, and to quote our notorious TV star turned President, tell them, "You're FIRED!"

Doesn't that sound like fun? That will be a GREAT day for America!   We can all gather and throw a gigantic street party in front of the Capitol as they leave.

In order to become candidates, prospects will have to commit to several things.

First, to make our top priorities as newly-elected members of Congress to fix things that are badly broken.   That will include passing immediate legislation with serious election funding reform, passing immediate legislation severely limiting or nullifying the influence of special interest lobbyists altogether, doing whatever is needed to eliminate the earmarking process and to taking control over the regulatory powers of federal agencies and enforce Congressional oversight.

If we accomplish that and that is ALL that gets done, then all of this will be worthwhile.

Second, our candidates must commit to fully and wholeheartedly promote the entire legislative agenda developed in this process.

I believe it will also be prudent to promise a moratorium, a temporary halt, on ALL regulatory abilities of all Federal Agencies and a review of every one of the various regulatory agency rules passed in the past four or five years, seeking to eliminate all but the ones that actually serve the public interest.

Also, I think it will be necessary and appropriate to promise that every single item in the federal budget will be scrutinized with the same intent.

Those two tasks, by themselves, will no doubt save American taxpayers billions and billions of dollars.

But these are just ideas.   They are simply a starting point for our discussions and potential platform.   As we go through this process together, we will share and discuss many ideas.

Remember, NONE of this will get done without a HUGE, overwhelming majority, and the best way to secure that majority is to just decide to replace every single person we can replace in one election cycle.

Realistically, I understand that the likelihood of a clean sweep is a minute, but that does not make it impossible. Near the end of the last Presidential campaign, odds were VERY high that the winner would NOT win.   Yet, he did. People do win lotteries, improbabilities do occur, Roger Bannister did run a sub-4-minute mile, the Cubs did win a World Series, and sometimes all the forces just align and amazing things happen.   A clean sweep represents the best assurance we have of making this work, so that is the goal, 468 OUT THE DOOR in 2020.

This is potentially the most challenging political goal in all of human history, but that IS the objective of our middle class revolution - sweep 468 Congressional seats in the 2020 election!

Sounds crazy I know, but so did sailing around the world when most thought it was flat.   So did the idea of powered flight, until the Wright Brothers showed us it could be done.

If I had told you 20 years ago that today we would be walking around with a phone in our pocket that could connect us to virtually anyone in the world, that we could use the same device to take and send pictures and movies to virtually anyone, watch TV, listen to the radio, read the daily news for every city on the planet, find our exact location and give us directions to anywhere we want to go, handle all our banking business, pay our bills, and much, much more... I would have been labeled an absolute lunatic, yet I'll wager that every one of us and every member of our household over the age of ten has just such a device, and uses it all the time!

I just want all of us to understand and believe, WE CAN DO THIS.   The American middle class has NEVER backed away from a big challenge before.   If this does not get done, we will have no one to blame but ourselves, and whatever fate awaits will be of our own choosing.

I do want to voice one caveat.   I have no delusions that mine is a perfect plan.   It will not magically solve all our problems.   Even if it works, governing will still be a massively complex responsibility.   Government will never make everyone happy.   However, it IS a plan and it WILL solve a lot of problems within our government, both short-term and long-term.   Most importantly, it will fix enough problems to allow our government to self-correct when needed, and allow it to be more responsive to the needs of the American public.

As I look out over the political landscape, I simply can't find another plan to work with.   I hear plenty of complaints.   I can and have walked into a room and said out loud that I think we should just "fire them all and start over" (speaking of Congress), and nearly everyone in the room voices hearty approval. It seems everyone likes the idea.   I hear a lot of talk and wishful thinking, but no real plan.   So if we really want change, we need to give serious consideration to these ideas and grant a little grace to the shortcomings. This idea seems to be the only other game in town.

The REAL question is, do we really want change?   Have we actually had enough and are we ready to insist on better? Or are we just going to sit back and do nothing and let the status quo run its course?

The goal here is to make our government WORK for us, ALL of us, and implement improvements that allow us to fix it when it is not functioning properly without having to do a complete overhaul again.

In the 2020 elections, I want to give voters some real, solid, well-defined choices, and try to offer enough benefits that a political tidal wave will show up at the polls and support our candidates.

THIS is a government OF the people, BY the people and FOR the people.   Cool concept, huh? Mr. Lincoln was really on to something!

You may be asking by now just where we would find these candidates.   Well, it will be quite a task, but if we put together the right package of ideas, this will be the easiest part.   Candidates are everywhere.   We have an abundance of intelligent, articulate, passionate, patriotic, honest, hard-working people who would see this as an act of service for their country.   People who fit that description abound all over America.   The middle class is loaded with those of us who want to make a difference: Teachers, first responders, soldiers, truck drivers, health care professionals, small business owners, store managers, even students who meet the respective age requirements to hold office, people from all walks of life.   I believe integrity, intelligence, and patriotism are alive and well outside of Washington, and when we have the ideas refined and big enough to excite the electorate, we will be able to find candidates.

So, instead of sending a few or even a lot of new faces to Washington in an election cycle and hoping for change, only to have our hopes sucked into the existing quagmire to disappear in the Washingtonian sludge, WE decide on laws we want to be passed before the election and WE send an overwhelming contingent people to Washington to pass them.

If we REALLY want to change our Congress and make it work, we have to change our thinking.   We need a new set of expectations and a fresh perspective.

We all know, at some level, that "if we keep doing what we are doing, we will keep getting what we are getting," right?

Well, when we go vote, we typically vote for an individual representative.   Our vote is not a vote for or against Congress as a whole, it is for an individual, and one we think will best represent OUR interests and maybe help create change.

If we are going to change Congress, the only possible way I see to make that happen is to vote AGAINST CONGRESS. We have to change our perspective from voting for an individual to voting for or against Congress as a unit.

There have been times in recent history where we have replaced well over a hundred Congressional members in one election.   Did that solve the problems we have with Congress?   No.   Why?   Because CONGRESS is broken. The entire system is broken: the election process, the lawmaking process, the governing process, the accountability process are ALL broken.   The entire system is mired in greed and promoting self-interests at every turn.

Have you noticed that very often, when a fast food chain or large chain of convenience stores wants to remodel their building, they just bulldoze away the existing structure and start over?   It's often much faster and easier to start from scratch and build a new one than it is to upgrade the old one.

Well, I believe that describes where we are with Congress. Our Congress is like a house with plumbing problems, electrical problems, HVAC problems, structural problems, broken windows, a sagging foundation, severe termite damage, and a terribly leaky roof.

It's time to get a whole new house.

The ONLY way we will build a whole new Congress is if we are willing to put America before ourselves.   When it comes time to vote, we must be willing to forego voting for representatives that may support our own self- interests, and decide to vote for one who will fix big problems within our government.   We can pursue self interests again in subsequent elections, but if we don't the fix the problems while we can, we may not have that option later.

Understanding that, if we are sure we want change, the place to start is to decide to vote for change; meaning that we decide we will not keep doing what we are doing.   In this case, it means deciding that we WILL NOT keep voting like we are voting.

If we go to the voting booth thinking, "well most of the other representatives will be voted out, but I like MY representative, so I'm going to vote for him or her again," then we vote for the status quo, and guess what? NOTHING changes.

So the very first step to make in changing Congress is to go to our website, MiddleClassRevolution.net, and sign the pledge that in the 2020 elections, WE WILL vote for change. We are not asking that you pledge any money.   The pledge won't cost you a cent.   But it will serve as a stepping stone that will allow us all to say, "I have made my choice. I am moving forward and not looking back."

The pledge is simply a promise to ourselves and to fellow Americans that in the 2020 election we WILL vote and make our voices heard, and we WILL NOT vote for anything that supports the status quo.   That helps us mentally close the door on doing what we have been doing and commits us to change and to building a better future for all of us.

If you will make that pledge, I will promise my very best efforts to make sure that regardless of where you live, you will have someone on the ballot that will support our entire agenda.

The next step will be to get involved with the idea exchange and discussion.   Help up put together a platform that will get this done. Participate online and in our actual town hall meetings when they come to your area.

The fourth step will be to help spread the word.   Talk to everyone who will listen, and right now, almost no one is happy with Congress and starting that conversation is really easy to do.   Let them know we have a plan, a real plan for change and that we can make it happen.

The final step will be so show up at the polls in November 2020 and cast your vote for the middle class revolution.

So there is my plan.   I hope you like it.

In some ways, this plan looks like a political party on steroids, but it is NOT a political party.   There is no plan to continue to function as a party, or even at all after the 2020 election cycle.   My plan is a one shot deal.   If it works, then what comes after will follow its natural course.   If America wants a third major party, we will have a good start.   Republicans and Democrats will still exist in large numbers, and will still battle over respective ideologies through election cycles.   The real benefit will be, if we make this plan work, that our government will once again be a representative, functioning government.

If we can sweep out the old and change the way Washington works and make it functional again, all who so choose, and I believe that will be most, will simply return to regular, normal lives, vacating Washington but leaving it a much better place.   The people I believe we have to find and elect are not people who are or have any desire to become lifelong politicians.   However, it is quite conceivable that if we make government functional again, constituents will not want our candidates to leave!   That will ultimately be left to the candidate and their voters.

That my friends is what a democracy, what government of the people, by the people and for the people looks like to this average Joe.

We can make it work, and I believe if the middle class is to survive and thrive, we MUST get it done. Will you help me in my crazy quest?

I hope this is an idea all of us can not only support but grow to love and about which we will become passionate, excited and engaged.   I believe our country's future is riding on it.

CHAPTER 10 - "LET'S ROLL"

So, here is the choice I see being offered by our Middle Class Revolution.

Stay with the status quo and get:

- A rich Congress supported by an even richer group of people who are obsessed with acquiring more wealth and power, regardless of the cost or impact on most Americans
- A diminished and weakening middle class with far superior numbers whose voice is drowned out by the wealthy minority
- A broken Congress whose primary interest and main function is getting themselves re-elected
- A Congress that has no real idea of the challenges of the middle class
- A Congress that has no clue of what it is like to be poor, and has no real interest in eliminating poverty
- A Congress that models selfishness, stubbornness and division to all Americans
- A Congress that is incredibly corrupt, who continues to sell out the best interest of our current and future generations for the sake of their own selfish and greedy ambition
- A Congress that has virtually NO chance of EVER balancing the federal budget, much less of reducing the national debt.
- A Congress that has abdicated their responsibilities and delegated those responsibilities to a bureaucratic army of regulators with absolutely no Congressional oversight.

- A Congress that regularly use personal earmarks and special spending projects to hold the American taxpayer hostage to pet programs to aid in re-election campaigns.
- A Congress from whom you have no idea what to expect, when or if important issues will be discussed, nor what the outcomes may be (except that you can expect more of the same)

Vote for change:

- Elect an entire Congress made up of people from the middle class who have no agenda except to do what is best for the largest possible number of people.
- Elect an entire Congress committed to assisting and expanding the middle class and improving the opportunities offered to America's middle class.
- Elect a vibrant, new Congress committed to fixing long-term problems without the influence of either self-serving ambition or the myriad of outside special interests that currently determine what laws get passed.
- Elect an entire Congress that have no plans to become career politicians or even to be re-elected, but simply want to serve their country, fix what is broken, and then go back to their regular lives.
- Elect an entire Congress far more likely to understand what it is like to be poor and who are committed to helping move as many people out of poverty as possible.

- Elect an entire Congress willing and anxious to talk about solutions instead of personal agendas.
- Elect an entire Congress that comes to Washington from grassroots, community support and has no ties to either political bosses, wealthy donors or any big-business interests.
- Elect an entire Congress that is not already corrupted by Washington politics, pledges to restore honesty and transparency to our government, and is committed to a written plan to institute and enforce ethical practices and offer safeguards against future political corruption.
- Elect an entire Congress having a specific plan, committed to writing, to solve some of America's most pressing problems, including balancing the national budget,   reducing the national debt plus a whole lot more.
- Elect an entire Congress that has clearly explained to us exactly what to expect, drawn up a specific plan, and have sworn on video and on paper to support that plan word for word.
- Elect an entire Congress that pledges to halt all regulations being issued by regulatory agencies that have no Congressional oversight; to review all the regulations issued in the last five years and to eliminate all but those necessary for the best interest of our nation; and to establish and mandate Congressional oversight of these agencies in the future.
- Elect an entire Congress that promises to have the federal budget reviewed line by line, and to eliminate any spending that does not serve the overall good of the nation.

- Elect an entire Congress that is willing to work for the best interest of our country, and in the process, show the world how to both be respectful of the views of others and still fully support the values of the American people to promote, life, liberty and the pursuit of happiness throughout our nation.
- Elect an entire Congress that is both willing and committed to making elections fair, limiting campaign contributions and the undue influence of the very wealthy, and legislating massive campaign funding reform.
- Elect an entire Congress that is both willing and committed to limiting the access of professional lobbyists to gain special favor and influence among our elected officials.
- Elect an entire Congress that is committed to holding itself and future Congresses to the highest possible standard of ethics.

Seems like a pretty simple choice to me.   I hope we agree!

Now the naysayers and critics will no doubt make a big deal of our team having no experience and will claim that this inexperienced crowd is not qualified or capable of managing such a daunting task.

That is pure B.S.

The founding fathers of our nation didn't have any experience governing, but were smart, passionate and wanted what was best for our country, and it worked.   Our candidates will have those same characteristics, and it will work again.   There will no doubt be some stumbles, and implementation of our changes may progress slowly at first, but I have NO doubt we can accomplish these goals and more.

Besides, we probably have more collective governing experience filling the halls of our Congress than perhaps any organization in the history of mankind, and look what it has gotten us.   We KNOW if we keep supporting the way things are being done that we are going to continue to get EXACTLY what we have been getting.   To think otherwise is pure lunacy. We don't know if a whole new crew can do any better, but the odds are pretty good we can't do any worse.

For the middle class, I sincerely believe it is "do or die." We have few options other than accepting whatever fate the ultra rich decide for us if we do not make some real changes while we can.

And just as a bonus to this whole idea, wouldn't it be terrific if, when the dust is all settled,   we get to feel that we could actually trust our government?   I mean, the default thinking right now is the old joke, "How do you tell if a politician is lying?" "His lips are moving!"   That is what we have come to expect.   That is how low we have set the bar for people who govern our country.   Wouldn't it be great if, when members of Congress said something, we could have the expectation that it was actually the truth?

Isn't it time we made ethics relevant again on Capitol Hill? Is there ANY chance it can be done with the current crowd? Here is a famous quote from the TV personality, Dr. Phil. "The best indicator of future behavior is past behavior."   If that is true, and I believe it is, that precludes virtually any chance of Washington changing the way things work, and total lack of ethics is how things currently work.

Do we have a better chance of reinstating ethics with the crowd that is there, or with a whole new crowd brought in from hard-working, middle class America? Seems like a no-brainer to me.

Joining the Middle Class Revolution is the only real alternative I see to continuing what we are doing.

So, if we agree and want to start the wheels of change to turn in our favor, what can we do?

For now, I think the best place to start is just to go to our website, MiddleClassRevolution.net, and do a few simple things.

The first step is a crucial one, and that is simply get on our mailing list. As this project progresses, things will change and information will flow quickly. Our email list is one of the core tools we will use for keeping everyone informed and up to date.

The other primary tool we will use to effect change is our website. Obviously, as we move forward there will be a LOT to do, and our website will be the gathering place. It is where much of our work will be explained and executed. Book mark it, then visit our site often and choose to get involved. You will have plenty of options.

Take our surveys. Attend our webinars. Give us feedback. Volunteer. Participate in the process. If we don't make change a priority, and become involved in forcing change to take place, then we all just lose, period. And if we lose, it looks to me like it will be pretty final.

Resistance will be formidable, and the further down the road we get, the more resistance we will encounter. No doubt, cruel and hateful things will be said about us and what we are trying to do. But if we want to save the middle class, we have to rally together and ignore the resistance.

We have to remember that regardless of how well we may like our current legislators, and regardless of whatever promises come from Washington, the status quo WILL NOT be changed from the inside. If we really want change, the current Congress has to go! We simply must vote for candidates and an agenda that are completely fresh and different.

And don't worry, if we do what we need to do in the interim, when the 2020 elections arrive, there will be other viable and preferable choices on every ballot.

Another simple thing we all can do is just talk to people about real political change. Get as many people involved in the discussion as possible. Then talk about our plan. Let everyone know there is a new, viable option on the table.

There are plenty of interested individuals around if we just start a conversation about the project. I am sure we will all be amazed at what happens by simply saying in a small group of people, "I think we should FIRE THEM ALL!" Then if we follow up with, "and I know how to actually get it done," trust me, conversation from there will be easy. We will make immediate friends!

Use your social media connections to open conversation and create interest. Remember, currently 84% of Americans are unhappy with Congress. That is seven out of eight. Those are pretty good odds. There are plenty of people anxious to express frustration with Congress.   Just open a conversation and talk honestly.

Also, something everyone can do that will help us continue to spread our message is to order bumper stickers and vinyl graphics from our site.   T-shirts, signs and other promotional tools will be available soon.   These will help us spread the word about our goal and support this idea as it grows and the revenue will give us more options to keep spreading the word.   And just as importantly, the attention generated by bumper stickers, windshield graphics, t-shirts and more will also help stimulate interest and discussion about empowering and revitalizing the middle class.

Finally, at the risk of sounding mercenary, it would be very helpful to tell everyone we can about my book.   Since these are my ideas, I am likely one of the best advocates available for the ideas discussed here, and I would love to be able to get out of the seat of my truck and promote our middle-class revolution full time.   That means persuading lots of people to buy and read my book.

My goal for the moment is to start to generate momentum and buzz, that is, to get the idea of actually firing the entire Congress at one time circulating and have people talking about it.

As we progress, there will undoubtedly be a need for volunteers, and we will have many opportunities for lots of people to assist.   I personally think it would be wonderful if we created an entire subculture of political activism and bring as many voices as possible into the political process. Is that not, after all, what government of, by and for the people should actually look like?

So there they are: My ideas on how to mount a desperately needed middle-class revolution! This is my very best effort to clearly identify and define a very troubling problem, outline the details of a potential solution, and share some simple steps that can be taken to begin the initiative to change the status quo.

Now, my concerns and ideas, and the fate or our middle class are collectively in our hands. All I can do now is ask for your help to get it going.

So, if we agree that this is important and that we have to get this off to a strong start, then please visit the MiddleClassRevolution.net website TODAY, right now, in fact. Pause what you are doing for just a moment, and use your phone or your computer to go to our website, get on our mailing list, and let's get started. The longer we wait, the more likely we are to sit back and settle for things continuing as they are.

If we are going to make this happen, we need to create some buzz and momentum so I'll close with the now immortal words of Todd Morgan Beamer, spoken as probably the last words of a true American hero on September 11, 2001..."Let's roll!"

www.ingramcontent.com/pod-product-compliance
Lightning Source LLC
Chambersburg PA
CBHW072213280526
45788CB00002B/1003